THE LONDON
BUS GUIDE

The Routes ~ The Buses
The Garages ~ The Companies

C000226163

CONTENTS

Hackney Central 38

LT12 GHT

Foreword

From time to time manufacturers will send demonstrator vehicles to the London Operators for evaluation. One such vehicle is Wrightbus Streetlite, DRZ 9420, which has been trialled by several operators. During July 2012 it was in Enfield working for Arriva. *Photo: Peter Horrex*

The first edition of this guide, published in September 2011 has proved extremely popular, the comments we have received have been very complimentary and therefore it shouldn't have come as a surprise that it sold out so quickly.

It was always planned to make the guide an annual release, the London bus scene is constantly changing and this is reflected in this totally revised second edition.

For those who bought the first edition, you know what to expect, for those who missed out...

The purpose of this guide is to explain the operation of Transport for London's (TfL) bus routes and to make your visit to the capital more rewarding and enjoyable. The book is designed to be taken out and used as a quick reference guide when you visit the London area, so the information is presented in a way we find useful when visiting locations for the first time. With this in mind, your feedback will be welcomed so we can modify and improve future editions.

There is one proviso: Because of the nature of London bus operations (and despite our best

efforts to provide an accurate picture), you need to be aware that the scene is constantly changing. What you see today may be completely different tomorrow. The information is correct to 16th September 2012 and we have also highlighted future changes, where known, on the opening page of the relevant section. However, no book can hope to give you every quirky little detail. You need to get out and explore for yourself. We hope this book provides a significant nudge in the right direction.

I must also thank the following:

David Maxey for supplying some of the detailed information. The photograhers who've plugged the gaps in our photo collection and the garage staff who've patiently answered our endless questions this year.

I hope you find this book useful in your exploration of London.

Ken Carr
Boreham, Essex,
September 2012

London Bus Network Overview

The London network is unique in Britain in that it's the only one to be regulated. The buses are organised by TFL's subsidiary London Bus Services Ltd, trading as London Buses (LB). It is this body that decides which routes are run and the service levels to be operated. LB also monitors service quality and is responsible for bus stations, bus stops, fares, revenue protection, radio and vehicle tracking equipment, roadside staff to deal with diversions and major incidents, and the marketing of the London network.

More than 700 routes are operated and more than 100 of those are 24-hour, 7 days a week. Incidentally this is the best night route network in the world. In addition, 600-series routes provide morning and afternoon school journeys in term time, and a declining number of mobility services (900-series routes) operate once a week.

Since the year 2000, there has been a dramatic increase in London bus usage. During the last year, over 2.3 billion passengers were carried and they travelled 490 million kilometres. This is an increase of 3/4 billion passengers since 2001/2; quite remarkable.

Contracts

Bus services within the TfL area are operated by private companies under contract to London Buses. Contracts are awarded route by route, normally for a period of five years. However, under the Quality Incentive (QI) scheme, there is an option to extend each route's contract by two years. As the name suggests, the aim is to incentivise operators to provide quality service during the core contract period. Although routes are generally tendered individually, others in the same area often come up for renewal at the same time to make changeovers easier.

The tendering programme is continuous, with between 15% and 20% of the network typically offered each year. Tender evaluation focuses on best value for money, but also takes into account safety and quality as essential features. Contract payments are directly linked to the mileage each route runs and to the overall reliability of the service. Comprehensive quality measurements are in place across all aspects of delivery.

Before offering a tender, London Buses reviews each route to produce a service specification detailing the route that buses will take (including terminal arrangements), service frequency at different times of day and on different days of the week (including the times of first and last buses), and the type and capacity of vehicle to be used. Operators are then asked to provide a schedule for delivering the specified level of service, along with the base cost of meeting this level plus a profit margin.

Although London Buses operates an approved supplier list, it routinely places advertisements in the Official Journal of the European Union seeking expressions of interest from potential operators.

Once a new applicant has been assessed and approved, it is then able to compete in the route-by-route tendering process. Invitations to Tender (ITTs) are issued every 2-4 weeks.

Route sizes vary considerably, as does each route's Peak Vehicle Requirement (PVR). This is the number of buses required to operate the service at times of greatest frequency - usually the morning and evening 'rush hours', but not exclusively so - and it ranges from one to more than fifty. Services are classified as either High Frequency (5 buses or more per hour throughout much of the week) or Low Frequency (4 buses per hour or fewer). About 82% of the network is High Frequency. The highest frequency routes have a bus every 2-3 minutes, the lowest frequency have only a single return journey each day. Most routes operate from about 04.30 till midnight, but an increasing number run 24 hours a day. Some routes 'morph' into night bus services between midnight and 04.30 (87 becomes N87, for example) with their daytime routes extended or modified.

Within the tender documentation, London Buses also specifies the minimum requirements for the vehicles to be used. The operator may choose the vehicle manufacturer, so long as its vehicles meet the criteria in the specification (like potential operators, new bus models are individually assessed and approved by TfL). Tenders are submitted on a sealed bid basis and must contain all relevant information for London Buses to make an effective evaluation.

The award of Contracts is based on achieving the most economically advantageous outcome within the resources available. The criteria include:

Price Ability - to deliver quality services to the levels specified in the ITT.

Staffing Ability - to recruit, train and retain personnel of a suitable calibre.

Premises - the suitability of an existing depot, and/or the operator's ability to obtain a suitable depot.

Vehicles - the type proposed and any additional features they offer above the tender specification. The operator's ability to maintain vehicles in an acceptable condition throughout the life of the contract is a major consideration.

Financial Status - the operator's resources to fund start-up costs and provide stability over the contract term.

Schedules - compliance with the specifications.

Tender evaluation is led by a Contracts Tendering Manager supported by a small team of skilled technical and commercial staff. Recommendations for contract awards are discussed and approved by the Tender Evaluation Committee, comprising the directors of London Bus Services Ltd.

As mentioned above, there is a nominated gross cost attached to each contract (operating costs plus profit), but the Quality Incentive aspect also provides for performance bonuses and/or deductions, as well as the two-year extension option. Each contract also has a specified Minimum Performance Standard reflecting the particular characteristics of the route. Performance monitoring data obtained by London Buses is normally shared with the operator. The contract price is adjusted each year in line with inflation.

The Quality Incentive scheme and performance monitoring are inextricably linked, covering not only service reliability but also driving quality and vehicle condition. The latter two are monitored by a combination of 'mystery traveller' surveys and vehicle inspections at garages. All of this is combined in a set of 'extension threshold' criteria in the tender documentation which, if met, trigger the automatic two-year extension. The operator can choose to decline, in which case the route would be re-tendered immediately at the end of the contract. In the event of acceptance, the extension is on the same basis as the original contract and the route is removed from the tendering renewal process for two years.

Although operators are expected to deliver the full contracted service, this is not always possible. Mechanical breakdowns, staff sickness, roadworks, road closures and other incidents on or near the route can all have a negative effect, hence the minimum performance standard. Any mileage which cannot be operated is split into two categories: Deductible Lost Mileage (loss of route operation considered to be within the Operator's reasonable control, e.g. staff absence, mechanical breakdown) and Non-Deductible Lost Mileage (instances beyond the Operator's reasonable control, such as adverse traffic conditions). Obviously, the Operator is not paid for Deductible Lost Mileage, and the deduction is calculated on a *pro rata* basis. Not surprisingly the operators and TfL have teams of people who monitor the reasons for lost mileage.

The London Dial-a-Ride service is upgrading from Mercedes-Benz mini-buses to Volkswagen T5 Bluebird Tuscanas. These are 6.8 metre vehicles licensed to carry eight passengers. One of over 200 to be introduced since 2008, D7162, passes through Golders Green. *Photo: Madeleine Carr*

London's environmental issues and poor air quality have been rapidly climbing the list of priorities for tender assessment in recent years. New vehicles have to conform to the latest European emissions standards and operators are also encouraged to introduce higher standards sooner than European law requires. Buses operating on the London network have a minimum standard of Euro-4 which came into effect from 3rd January 2012. Since late 2009, new vehicle engines for London's buses have been manufactured to Euro-5 standard and there is already an Enviro400 operating in the capital for Abellio which is Euro-6 standard. Each of these progressive steps relates (in the main) to the effectiveness of the vehicles' diesel particulate filters.

With pollution in mind (and the constant threat of heavy fines being imposed by the EU) Transport for London is trialling the latest advances in vehicle technology, including a batch of hydrogen fuel cell buses which produce *no* polluting emissions. Diesel-electric hybrids (powered by smaller engines coupled to generators and batteries charged by regenerative braking) also produce lower emissions than a traditional diesel bus. Over 300 of varying designs are now in service - a figure expected to reach 450 by March 2013. In addition, London Mayor Boris Johnson has pledged to deliver 600 of the New Bus for London (NBfL) hybrid design by April 2016.

Other Services

London Buses also procures buses for rail replacement journeys on behalf of London Underground. More than 100 such contracts are issued in advance of planned engineering work each year. Some involve only a single bus, others can require fifty. The tendering process is similar to that used for normal services and front-line operators such as First Group and Abellio regularly win these contracts. Smaller companies currently without TfL routes, such as Ensign also supply vehicles for this work.

London Buses' Dial-a-Ride service is run for the benefit of disabled and elderly people. The service initially used a fleet of Mercedes-Benz minibuses but these are rapidly being replaced by a fleet of Bluebird Tuscanas painted in the familiar TfL Red and owned by London Buses itself. Booking one is similar to booking a taxi, although the passenger has to pre-register before being able to use the service. He or she can then phone a call centre with details of the journey they wish to make and they're given a pick-up time, varying 15 minutes either way. However, they may have to share a vehicle with other passengers on a journey likely to involve pick-ups & set-downs for others. For this reason, there is no guarantee the route will be direct, but the service is free and a commendable addition to London Buses' operations.

The Go-Ahead company in London runs a Commercial Services Fleet, with a variety of older

The Wartime London tour was introduced in 2012, it runs on Tuesdays, Thursdays & Saturdays between April & October. Operated by Evans Tours in conjunction with Ensignbus it uses one of the latter's vintage RTs. RT8 stands in Vauxhall Bridge Road before operating the afternoon tour. *Photo: Ken Carr*

bus types including the much-loved Routemaster. These buses are available for general hire and also appear on special services linked to some of London's big annual events like the Chelsea Flower Show and the Wimbledon Tennis Championships. Regular members of the fleet, identifiable by their gold numbers, are augmented at busy times by vehicles of similar type (like the PVL class) normally engaged on TfL contracts.

A number of sightseeing-tours operate in the capital. The Original Tour (run by Arriva) and The Big Bus company are the largest. Each uses a mix of older types alongside recently-acquired, purpose-built, tri-axle buses from the Far East. Golden Tours moved into the Central London sightseeing market in the summer of 2011, using a small fleet of ALX400s and some new vehicles.

In addition to the big players, smaller, self-contained operations exist. On three days each week Ensignbus sends out one of its 'heritage' RTs on a wartime-themed tour. The Harrods store's open-top Routemasters appear on trips operated by Premium Tours, and in the evening Ghost BusTours' black RML runs a 'scary' trip around London.

Countdown screens fitted to an increasing number of bus shelters provide 'next bus due' information for all routes serving the stop.

iBus

Every bus operating a TfL route is fitted with the Automatic Vehicle Location (AVL) system, better known as iBus. It works using a combination of technologies, including the Global Positioning System (GPS) and 'map matching', which receives input from a gyroscope and the bus's speedometer/odometer.

The iBus room at Plumstead garage. A bus data radio fitted to each bus uses GPS to send information on its location to the operators computer terminals, this information is then used to improve service reliability via a direct link to the driver. *Photo: Ken Carr*

The bus data radio uses GPS to send its location to a central computer system approximately every 30 seconds. This information is available to service controllers monitoring performance along the route and enables them to take action to improve service reliability. It is not uncommon to hear drivers receiving radio messages from controllers instructing them to wait time at a stop to reduce the 'bunching' that can occur when traffic conditions are bad. As well as the driver-generated adjustments, TfL can also send instructions directly to traffic lights, altering the timing of their phases to help speed up buses when congestion occurs.

The bus's on-board computer carries the details of every stop along the route and all of the possible destinations. The computer constantly tracks the bus's position from the AVL information and announces each stop as it occurs, using pre-recorded 'sound bites'. Digital displays on both decks convey the same information to the hearing-impaired. Important locations close to stops, such as hospitals, are also announced visually and aurally.

Centre Comm - London Buses' 24/7 Emergency Command and Control Centre - can also use the bus PA system to communicate directly with passengers in the event of an emergency. Similarly, the driver can make contact with Centre Comm if an accident occurs, allowing the incident to be pin-pointed precisely when emergency assistance is despatched.

The central computer system also predicts the time it will take for buses to arrive at stops. Each bus's arrival can then be displayed on LED countdown indicators at key bus shelters. This 'real time' system is now installed at more than 2,000 locations. The latest development allows passengers to check bus information in real time on their smart-phones.

As a continual process, iBus also provides detailed journey data which operators can use to improve individual routes.

Ticketing

All fares revenue goes directly to TfL and fares are collected in a number of ways. London buses accept Travelcards, Oyster Card products, bus passes and single journey cash fares. The latter used to be charged on length of journey (based on fare stages), but there is now only one flat fare. From 2000, this became higher for journeys in Zone 1 than in outer zones, but the difference was eliminated in 2004 with the introduction of Oyster Card flat fares. Cash fares are considerably higher than Oyster fares for the same journey.

With the Oyster Card 'pay as you go' (formerly Pre-Pay), users are charged a fixed amount for single journeys, but a 'daily cap' limits the maximum deducted from the balance on a card, regardless of how many buses are used that day (a day is measured from 04.30 to 16.30). Weekly

Note: TfL plans to phase out the roadside ticket machines within the next twelve months. When this happens, only valid passes, Day Travelcards and Oyster will be accepted on bus services running within the 'cashless zone'.

For the Enthusiast . . .

London has lots to offer (lots of buses for one thing) and there are a number of 'hot spot' locations where you can enjoy a wide variety of types. If you have never been to central London before, the area between Trafalgar Square and Aldwych is especially recommended. At the latter location, for instance, you can see (on a good day) hydrogen fuel cell buses running alongside heritage Routemasters and many of the standard Alexander Dennis and Wrightbus models. In addition Victoria & Hyde Park Corner (especially if you want to see the NBfL) are recommended as is Marble Arch. Please refer to the 'Buses' section of this book for what can be found where.

During the year, various organisations have 'road runs' featuring a variety of older buses retracing routes they served in the dim and distant past. It's also worth keeping an eye out for garage open-days. Metroline's Potters Bar garage open day in July is becoming an annual event. As well as the garage's regular types, a host of heritage buses visit and you can take free rides on them around the local area. Metroline usually holds a second open day during the year. Stagecoach also occasionally hold open days or opportunities to take a guided tour around West Ham, keep an eye out in the bus magazines for further details.

To enhance your London experience, we recommend the various bus route maps. TfL produces a set of five free maps - a central London version and the rest of the area split into four quadrants - north-east, south-west, et cetera. These are also very useful for tracing Overground and Underground railways through the London area. The TfL maps are available from larger Tube stations and Travel Information Centres like the one at Victoria main line station. They can also be downloaded from the web in PDF format. Go to: http://www.tfl.gov.uk/gettingaround/maps/buses/ and scroll to the bottom of the page.

Alternatively, you can buy a map, especially the one many enthusiasts swear by - Mike Harris's Greater London Bus Map for around £2.00. A Night Bus version is also available. Further information from: www.busmap.co.uk

and monthly passes can also be purchased and loaded onto an Oyster Card. On boarding the bus, the Oyster Card is held up to a 'reader' which registers the journey and deducts the fare from the credit balance on the card. The process repeats for subsequent journeys until the daily cap (currently £4.20 for buses only across all zones) is reached.

Children aged under 11 travel free; 11 to 15s travel free if they have an 11-15 Oyster photocard. Further concessions apply to those aged 16 to 18. Over-60s resident in London can apply for a Freedom Pass allowing free off-peak travel on buses and the rail network. A similar scheme is available to the disabled. Most over-60s living outside of London can apply for an English bus pass from their local authority. Since 2008, these passes have been accepted England-wide and provide free travel on all TfL routes after 9.30 am on weekdays and any time at weekends. *[Please note: If you are approaching your 60th birthday and plan to apply for one of these concessions, the age qualification is gradually being raised from 60 to 65 to save money. However, you are eligible immediately if you were born before 6th April 1950. There are similar schemes for residents of Scotland and Wales, but these passes are not accepted on TfL routes.]*

Cash customers travelling on Route W7 must buy tickets before boarding from the bus stop ticket machines. Many bus stops within the West End of London fall within a 'cashless area' designed to speed up the boarding process. The route numbers this requirement applies to are marked in yellow on bus stop displays along with 'Buy tickets before boarding'. Drivers on these routes do not issue tickets, passengers must have a valid ticket or pass before boarding. Outside the cashless area, single tickets (£2.30 as of Sept 2012) may be bought from the bus driver.

Further Reading

The London Omnibus Traction Society (LOTS) publishes an annual pocket-size book listing the fleet number and registration number of each bus, operator by operator. The 2012 version costs £6.50. Go to: www.lots.org.uk

British Bus Publishing publishes a London Bus Handbook. This A5 production is much heavier and glossier and includes garage allocations for each bus as well as plenty of colour photos. It retails at £18.25. See www.britishbuspublishing.co.uk for further information. However, this doesn't seem to be an annual publication, the latest was released in mid-2011.

LOTS is the main enthusiast society in the London area, which it covers in considerable detail in its monthly magazine The London Bus. This is available direct to your home in return for an annual membership fee of £22.00, or you can buy individual copies at places like the Ian Allan shops.

Further details from: LOTS, Unit N305, Westminster Business Square, 1-45 Durham Street, Vauxhall, London SE11 5JH or via the website: www.lots.org.uk

The PSV Circle reports monthly on the London bus scene via news sheets. A year's-worth costs £19.00 and you can start by visiting: www.psv-circle.org.uk

The Omnibus Society has a London Historical Research Group. Full details of this can be found at: www.Omnibussoc.org

While we're on the web, there are two other sites which are truly excellent.

The first - www.londonbusroutes.net - is a useful resource for the most recent/forthcoming changes.

The second - www.londonbusesbyadam.zenfolio.com - is a photo site with more than 13,000 images featuring every route in London.

The area covered by TfL is vast and there are plenty of rural spots, like this one which contrasts with the congestion of Central London. Scania OmniCity SP101 pulls away from a stop at Petersham on route 65 from Chessington World of Adventures. *Photo: Ken Carr*

The Operators

Although comparative calm has descended since the organised chaos provoked by bus deregulation, changes continue to occur from time to time in 'who operates what' in London.

The largest operator is Go-Ahead, with more than 23% of the total peak vehicle requirement. The increase over last year has mostly been prompted by the purchase in March 2012 of First Capital's Northumberland Park garage, its buses and routes. Go-Ahead is followed in size by Arriva with just under 20% of the cake. The smallest companies are CT Plus and Quality Line, both with less than 1%, while Sullivan Buses operates a soltary TfL route, the 298, which it won in February 2012 after deciding to re-enter the London market. Here are potted histories of the main companies, revealing the extent of worldwide financial interest in the running of London's buses.

Abellio is ultimately owned by the Nederlandse Spoorwegen of Holland, originally through its subsidiary NedRailways. In May 2009 the company bought Travel London (and the smaller Travel Surrey) from the National Express Group. Travel London came into being when NatEx bought the French-owned Connex Bus in 2004. A year later it bought Tellings-Golden Miller as well. After the most recent sale, the Travel London designation would

have been retained but for NedRailways changing it to Abellio Group in October 2009.

Arriva's first venture into London can be traced back to 1980 when the company was still known as Cowie, after the family who started the company in Sunderland in the 1930s. Cowie bought Grey-Green - basically a fast commuter coach service provider - in 1980. Seven years later, Grey-Green successfully tendered for some London routes. In 1994 the Cowie Group bought Leaside Buses, then the last LBL subsidiary, South London Transport. The group changed its name to Arriva in 1997. Further acquisitions followed - Kentish Bus in 1997, County Bus in 1998 and Londonlinks in 1999. Arriva has the distinction of having been the first to operate the bendibus in London and the last to operate Routemasters in normal daily service (as opposed to heritage). You may have noticed from other London bus publications that Arriva the Shires and Arriva Southern Counties Group (and their bus fleets) are listed separately from Arriva London. This is because they are separate companies operating from different Head Offices. Our book follows that convention.

First Group began operating London buses in 1997 when it acquired Centrewest. This was later followed by Capital Citybus, a former Hong Kong-based business bought out by local management, in

At Hammersmith, DE47, one of one hundred and twenty-eight 10.2m Enviro200s operating for the company, is followed by one of the company's thirty-two 10.5m Trident ALX400s TLA25. Both buses operate from Shepherd's Bush garage. *Photo: Peter Horrex*

1998. Both of these and operations in north London, now come under the First London banner.

Go-Ahead London is the collective name of the Go-Ahead Group's various operations in the capital. Based in Newcastle, its first London venture was the acquisition of London Buses Ltd. subsidiary London Central in September 1994. Another former LBL subsidiary, London General, which had initially been a management buy-out, was added in May 1996. The development of both companies since then has been on parallel lines but a shred of distinctiveness between them remains.

Metrobus was added to the London operation in September 1999. Formed in 1983 from the wreckage of the Orpington & District bus company collapse, Metrobus has retained a separate identity - so much so, that it is hard to discern any physical connection between Stockwell buses (London General) and Orpington buses apart from their (mostly) red colour. Go-Ahead expanded its London operation further in September 2006 when London General bought Docklands Buses. Eight months later, the group acquired the contracted bus operations of Blue Triangle but BT's MD, Roger Wright, understandably retained ownership of the heritage fleet. To complete the present shape of Go-Ahead London, the East Thames Buses brand was added in 2009 following a tendering process conducted by TfL.

The Go-Ahead London logo can be traced back to August 2008, although recent bus repaints have appeared with individual London General and London Central fleetnames beneath. There is also the vexed question of Go-Ahead's livery style, which somehow manages to dodge the 'buses must be red all over' edict issued by TfL.

London United was another LBL subsidiary subject to a management buy-out in 1994. Three years later, the French company Transdev bought it. Sovereign London was acquired in 2002 (re-named London Sovereign from 2004) via the convoluted route of Borehamwood Travel Services (original company name) Blazefield (whose Sovereign subsidiary bought BTS in 1994, whereupon the London tag was added) and Transdev, which bought the whole of Blazefield in 2006. In 2009 the Transdev Group began negotiations with Veolia Environnement with the aim of merging itself with Veolia Transport. In the resulting agreement, made in May 2010, it was agreed that the RATP Group, which had a minority shareholding in Transdev, would assume ownership of some of Transdev's routes and assets in lieu of cash payment. This had a considerable impact on Transdev's London operations, splitting the company into two unequal parts.

London Sovereign's two garages and their routes remained with Transdev as part of the merged Veolia Transdev group, RATP got everything else, i.e. the eight garages of what was originally London United. The agreement took effect in March 2011 and the London United name re-emerged alongside much-reduced RATP Group branding. The small number of buses operating London Sovereign routes still defiantly proclaim themselves to be Transdev.

In April 2012, RATP bought Epsom Coaches - a small, family-style firm which had moved into the bus market (rather than solely running coach tours) in the 1980s deregulation. It expanded into London routes in 1997. The bus operation was re-branded as Quality Line in 2003 and, since then, has

Over 700 of the 10.2m Enviro200 are running in London, most operators use them. London United operates one hundred and twenty-eight of them. DE107 awaits departure in Buckingham Palace Road. *Photo: Ken Carr*

TfL has decreed that London buses should be predominantly red all-over. However, the lure of advertisers' money means that some buses carry all-over advertising. During the summer of 2012 with the Olympics in town, the number treated this way rose dramatically. *Photo: Ken Carr*

gradually gained new contracts. The new acquisition operates as an independant division of RATP.

Metroline is another of the LBL companies from 1989, but acquired by the ComfortDelgro Group of Singapore in 2000. By then, Metroline had absorbed Atlas Bus (just after privatisation in 1994) London Northern and R&I Buses in 1998. ComfortDelgro has added Thorpes (2004) and Armchair (2005).

The **Stagecoach** Company's interest in London began in 1994 when it bought LB's East London Bus & Coach Company and the South East London & Kent Bus Company (known as Selkent). Stagecoach pulled out of London in 2006, surprisingly, when it sold its entire operation to the Australian Macquarie Bank for £263 million. The new owners reintroduced the East London and Selkent fleetnames and in 2009 created Thameside for its Rainham-based buses. In an equally surprising move, Stagecoach re-acquired the whole lot in October 2010 for only £59 million, whereupon Stagecoach branding was rapidly reinstated.

Hackney Community Transport was established in 1982 when 30 community groups in the London Borough of Hackney formed a pool of six vehicles with a grant from Hackney Borough Council, aimed at providing low cost van and minibus hire for those groups and a door-to-door alternative to public transport for the disabled. HCT gained its first TfL contract in 2001 to operate route 153 under the CT Plus brand. Further contracts followed in 2003. In July 2006 HCT merged with Lambeth and Southwark Community Transport, and in 2008 began running a bendibus

service to and from the Olympics 2012 site for construction workers.

Sullivan Buses re-entered the fray in February 2012 after winning the contract for route 298. From September 2012, the company started running a handful of TfL school bus routes. The company was formed in 1999 and currently runs routes in Hertfordshire, as well as rail replacement services for TfL.

Ensignbus also runs rail replacements contracts. Until 1990, the company had some London routes but sold them to Citybus. After a brief return, this came to an end again in 1999.

A brief word about 'livery', if that's the right word anymore. As mentioned in the Go-Ahead paragraph, operators running TfL-contracted routes must now paint their buses all-red, apart from modest fleet names. So, the distinctive blue skirts on the Metroline buses are gradually disappearing, as will the grey/yellow stripes on Go-Ahead's fleet, the 'grey sandwich' of Transdev, Arriva's white horns, and the swirls of First Group. The white London bus roundel is appearing on the all-over red buses. Apart from that, the only other embellishment is the word 'Hybrid' in green on the latest diesel-electrics, replacing the shower of green leaves on the earlier examples and the claim that they were all the Mayor of London's doing.

However, the reasoning behind the red all-over edict can be questioned as there seems to be no problem in covering some of London's buses in all-over advertising wraps.

Abellio

Abellio's main area of operation is South London. The 290 heads west from Twickenham to Staines. The driver has just changed the blinds of Enviro200, 8582 after its arrival at Staines bus station.
Photo: Ken Carr

Garages

QB	Battersea
BC	Beddington
TF	Fulwell
WS	Hayes
WL	Walworth

Fleet Total

688

Double Deckers - 385
Single Deckers - 303

PVR = 500

Head Office:
301 Camberwell New Road,
London, SE5 0TF

ROUTES OPERATED

3	35	40	100	112	117	152	156
157	172	188 24 hour	211	235	290	322	343
344 24 hour	350	381	407	414	434	452	455
481	484	490	931	969	C2 24 hour	C3	C10
H20	H25	H26	H28	N3	N35	N343	N381
P13	R68	R70	T33	U7	U9		

Single Deckers Operated

Dart - Nimbus
Dart - Pointer
Dart - Pointer 2
E20D - Enviro200 (E)
E200Dart - Enviro200
Electrocity

Double Deckers Operated

B7TL - Eclipse Gemini
E40D - Enviro400 (E)
E40D - Enviro400H (E)
Enviro400
Trident - ALX400

Not all of Abellio's routes stay south of the River Thames. To prove the point, ALX400, 9836 heads through Aldwych. This route is operated from Walworth garage. *Photo: Ken Carr*

Arriva

Garages

AE	Ash Grove
DX	Barking
CN	Beddington
BN	Brixton
CT	Clapton
TC	Croydon
DT	Dartford
E	Enfield
LV	Leeside Road
N	Norwood
AD	Palmers Green
SF	Stamford Hill
AR	Tottenham
TH	Thornton Heath
GR	Watford
WN	Wood Green

Fleet Total

1749

Double Deckers - 1405
Single Deckers - 344

PVR = 1310

Head Offices:
North: 16 Watsons Road, Wood Green N22 7TZ

South: Bus Garage, Brighton Road, Croydon CR2 6EL

Arriva is London's second biggest operator and is nominally split into two, Arriva North & Arriva South. The main area of operation is a central band that runs from north to south London. The company operates eighteen of these short SB120 Cadets from Thornton Heath garage for this route. *Photo Ken Carr*

ROUTES OPERATED

2	29	34	38	41	50	59	60
73	76	78	102 ⏱24 hour	109	121	123	125
128 ⏱24 hour	133	135	137	141	144	149 ⏱24 hour	150
159 ⏱24 hour	166	168	173	176 ⏱24 hour	184	192	194
197	198	221	242 ⏱24 hour	243 ⏱24 hour	250 ⏱24 hour	253	254
255	264 ⏱24 hour	279	289	307	312	313	317
318	319	325	327	329	341 ⏱24 hour	349	377
379	382	393	397	403	410	412	415
417	432	444	450	466	491	617	627
629	634	647	657	678	685	690	H1
N2	N29	N38	N41	N73	N76	N109	N133
N137	N253	N279	T31	W3	W6	W11	

Single Deckers Operated

Dart - ALX200 (ADL)
Dart - Pointer (PDL)
Dart - Pointer 2 (PDL)
E20D - Enviro200 (E) (EN/ENS/ENX)
E200Dart - Enviro200 (EN/ENL/ENS)
SB120 - Cadet (DWL/DWS)

Double Deckers Operated

B5LH - Eclipse Gemini 2 (HV)
B7TL - ALX400 (VLA)
B7TL - Eclipse Gemini (VLW)
DB250 - ALX400 (DLA)
DB250 - President (DLP)
DB250 - Pulsar Gemini (DW)
E40D - Enviro400 (E) (T)
Enviro400 (T)
Gemini 2 DL (DW)
Gemini 2 DL (E) (DW)
Gemini 2 HEV (HW)
New Bus for London (LT)

B7TL ALX400, VLA19 awaits the lights at Waterloo. 80% of Arriva's fleet is made up of double-deckers. Arriva (and its constituent companies) are the only London based operators to use the DAF DB250 chassis. It is found under ALX400, Gemini and President bodies. *Photo: Ken Carr*

Arriva Southern Counties

Garages

DT	Dartford
GY	Grays

Arriva Southern Counties comprises four smaller companies, two of which, Arriva Kent Thameside and Arriva Southend, have some TfL routes. An early DAF chassied Pulsar Gemini, 6216, based at Dartford in Kent, awaits its turn at the Bluewater shopping centre.
Photo: Ken Carr

Fleet Total

135

Double Deckers - 35
Single Deckers - 100

PVR = 109

Head Office:
Invicta House, Armstrong Road,
Maidstone, Kent ME15 6TY

ROUTES OPERATED

66	126	160	233	256	286	346	370
375	428	492	499	B12	B13	B15	

Dartford based SB120 short Cadets are used on the B13 & B15. *Photo: Ken Carr*

Arriva The Shires

Arriva The Shires runs both TfL and non-TfL routes. Red paint differentiates one batch of buses from the other. Six 7.8m Solos are based at Watford garage to work routes H1, H2 and H3 in the Golders Green area. *Photo: Ken Carr*

Garages

GR	Watford

Fleet Total

92

Double Deckers - 46
Single Deckers - 46

PVR = 71

Head Office:
487 Dunstable Road, Luton,
Bedfordshire LU4 8DS.

ROUTES OPERATED

142	258	268	288	303	305	340	640
642	H2	H3	H18	H19			

Single Deckers Operated

B6BLE - Crusader
Dart - Pointer
Optare Solo
SB120 - Cadet

Double Deckers Operated

DB250 - ALX400
DB250 Pulsar Gemini
Gemini 2 DL

A fleet of twelve DAF chassied Pulsar Geminis operates route 258. 6034 heads along College Road in Harrow. *Photo: Ken Carr*

CT Plus

Garages

HK   Ash Grove

Hackney Community Transport's CT Plus operates an interesting collection of single- and double-deckers. At present this route is operated by Darts with Nimbus bodies. However, from February 2013 these will be replaced by new buses. *Photo: Ken Carr*

Fleet Total

91

Double Deckers - 27
Single Deckers - 64

PVR = 69

Head Office:
Mare Street, South Hackney,
London E8.

ROUTES OPERATED

153	212	309	385	388	394	675	W5
W12	W13						

Single Deckers Operated

Dart - Nimbus (DCS/HDC)
Dart - Pointer (DPS)
E200Dart - Enviro200 (DA/DAS)
E200Dart - Esteem (DE)
Optare Alero (LF)
Optare Solo (OS)

Double Deckers Operated

Enviro400 - Olympus (EO)
N230UD - OmniCity (SD)
Trident - Myllenium Lolyne (HTL)
Trident - President (HTP)

Route 388 is normally operated with Lolynes, although the company's Presidents or its sole Olympus can appear. Here, HTL8 awaits another trip at the Mansion House stand at Blackfriars. *Photo: Ken Carr*

First

Route RV1 is operated by the 'hydrogen fuel-cell' buses alongside Enviro200s. DML44164 runs along Belvedere Road heading from Tower Hill to Covent Garden. *Photo: David Maxey*

Garages

ON	Alperton
AS	Atlas Road
DM	Dagenham
G	Greenford
HS	Hayes
LI	Lea Interchange
UX	Uxbridge
X	Westbourne Park
WJ	Willesden Junction

Fleet Total

1161

Double Deckers - 714
Single Deckers - 447

PVR = 882

Head Office:
3rd Floor, Block B, MacMillan House, Paddington, London W2 1TY

ROUTES OPERATED

9H	18	23 (24 hour)	25 (24 hour)	26	28	30	31
58	70	83 (24 hour)	92	95	165	179	187
193	195	206	207	223	224	226	228
236 (24 hour)	245	252	266 (24 hour)	282	295 (24 hour)	308	328
331	339	365 (24 hour)	368	427	487	498	607
608	646	648	652	656	667	679	686
953	A10	E1	E3	E5	E7	E9	E10
N18	N26	N28	N31	N207	RV1	U1	U2
U3	U4	U5	U10	W14	W15		

Single Deckers Operated

Dart - Capital (DM/DML/DMS)
Dart - Nimbus (DMC)
E200Dart - Enviro200 (DM/DML/DMS)
E20D - Enviro200 (E) (DM/DML/DMV)
SB200 - Pulsar 2 Hydrogen (WSH)
Streetlite DF (WM)

Double Deckers Operated

B7TL - Eclipse Gemini (VNW/VNZ)
B7TL - President (VNL)
B9TL - Eclipse Gemini 2 (VN)
B9TL - Eclipse Gemini 2 (E) (VN)
E40D - Enviro400 (E) (DN)
E40D - Enviro400H (E) (DNH)
Enviro400 (DN)
Gemini 2 HEV (WNH)
Gemini 2 DL (WN)
Routemaster (RM)
Trident - ALX400 (TNA)
Trident - President (TN/TNL)

Another Alperton bus, a Volvo B9TL Eclipse Gemini 2, 37793 passes Ealing Common. First have one hundred and ninety-one of this type running in London and they can usually be found on routes 18, 25, 58, 83, 295 and 427. *Photo: David Maxey*

Go-Ahead

Go-Ahead is the largest operator in London, made up of four companies, Blue Triangle, Docklands Buses, London Central & London General. Rainham garage's SE26 passes through Ilford. *Photo: Ken Carr*

Garages

BV	Belvedere
BX	Bexleyheath
Q	Camberwell
MW	Mandela Way
AL	Merton
NX	New Cross
NP	Northumberland Park
PM	Peckham
PL	Plough Lane
AF	Putney
BE	Rainham
SI	Silvertown
SW	Stockwell
A	Sutton
RA	Waterloo

Fleet Total

1526

Double Deckers - 1039
Single Deckers - 487

PVR = 1537

Head Office:
18 Merton High Strett, London
SW19 1DN

ROUTES OPERATED

1	11	12 *24 hour*	14 *24 hour*	19	20	21	22
24 *24 hour*	36 *24 hour*	37 *24 hour*	39	42	44	45	63
67	68	74	77	80	85 *24 hour*	87	88 *24 hour*
89	93 *24 hour*	108 *24 hour*	118	129	132	151	154
155	163	164	167	170	171	180	185
191	196	200	201	213 *24 hour*	219	225	229
231	244	249	259	270	276	280	299
300	315	321 *24 hour*	333	337	345 *24 hour*	347	355
357	360	362	363	364	376	389	399
401	413	422	424	425	430	436	453 *24 hour*
462	468	474 *24 hour*	476	485	486	493	507
521	549	616	621	624	625	639	649
650	651	655	658	661	669	670	673
692	699	B11	B16	D6	D7	D8	EL1 *24 hour*
EL2	G1	N1	N11	N19	N21	N22	N44
N63	N68	N74	N87	N89	N155	N171	N551
P5	P12	W4	W10	W16	W19	X68	

Single Deckers Operated

Citaro (MEC)
Dart - Capital (DMN)
Dart - Evolution (ED)
Dart - Pointer (DP/LDP)
Dart - Pointer 2 (LDP)
E20D - Enviro200 (SE/SEN)
E200Dart - Enviro200 (SE/SEN)
E200Dart - Esteem (SOE)
E200Dart - Evolution (ED)
Electrocity (WHY)
N94UB - East Lancs (ELS)
Optare Solo (OS)
SB120 - Cadet (DW)/DWL)

Double Deckers Operated

B5LH - Eclipse Gemini 2 (WHV)
B7TL - Eclipse Gemini (VWL/WVL)
B7TL - President (PVL/VP)
B9TL - Enviro400 (VE)
B9TL - Eclipse Gemini 2 (WVL)
E40D - Enviro400H (E) (EH)
Enviro400 (E)
Enviro400H (EH)
Enviro400 - Olympus (DOE)
Gemini 2 DL (WDL)
Gemini HEV (WHD)
N94UD OmniDekka (SO)
N230UD OmniCity (SOC)
Trident - President (PDN/PVN)

Go-Ahead operates forty-seven of the 10.6m B7TL Eclipse Gemini. Designated as VWLs, the shorter 10.1m variant is designated WVL. VWL 38, based at Mandela Way, passes through Waterloo on its journey from Tottenham Court Road. *Photo: Ken Carr*

London Sovereign

Garages

BT	Edgware
SO	Harrow

London Sovereign's main area of operation is North West London. One of the company's Dart Pointer 2s heads through Harrow on the H9 which is a circular route around the local area. *Photo: Ken Carr*

Fleet Total

163

Double Deckers - 65
Single Deckers - 98

PVR = 125

Head Office:
Busways House, Wellington
Road, Fulwell TW2 5NX

ROUTES OPERATED

13	114	183	251	292	324	398	605
H9	H10	H11	H13	H14	H17	N13	

Single Deckers Operated

Dart - Pointer 2 (DPS)
E200Dart - Enviro200 (DE/SDE)

Double Deckers Operated

B7TL - President (VLP)
B7TL - Vyking (VLE)
N94UD OmniDekka (SLE)
N230UD OmniCity (SP)

The only route that London Sovereign runs into Central London is this one from Golders Green. Any of the company's double-deckers can turn up on this working. At the bottom of Haymarket, Scania OmniDekka, SLE38, passes a broken down Humber. *Photo: Ken Carr*

London United

London United operates an interesting collection of buses. VP110, one of the dwindling number of centre-staircase B7TL Presidents, awaits its next trip in Twickenham. *Photo: Jack Marian*

Garages

FW	Fulwell
AV	Hounslow
HH	Hounslow Heath
PK	Park Royal
S	Shepherd's Bush
V	Stamford Brook
TV	Tolworth
NC	Twickenham

Fleet Total

915

Double Deckers - 540
Single Deckers - 375

PVR = 680

Head Office:
Busways House, Wellington
Road, Fulwell TW2 5NX

ROUTES OPERATED

9	10 (24 hour)	27 (24 hour)	33 (24 hour)	49	57 (24 hour)	65 (24 hour)	71
72 (24 hour)	81	94 (24 hour)	110	111 (24 hour)	116	120	131
148 (24 hour)	203	216	220 (24 hour)	222	265	267	272
281 (24 hour)	283	285 (24 hour)	371	391	419	423	440
482	613	665	671	681	691	696	697
698	965	C1	E11	H22	H32	H37	H91
H98	K1	K2	K3	K4	N9	N97	

Single Deckers Operated

Citaro
Dart - Pointer (DPK)
Dart - Pointer 2 (DP/DPS)
E200Dart - Enviro200 (DE/DLE/SDE)
E200Dart - Enviro200H (HDE)
Optare Tempo (OT)
Optare Versa (OV)

Double Deckers Operated

B7TL - ALX400 (VA)
B7TL - Eclipse Gemini (VR)
B7TL - President (VP)
B7TL - Vyking (VE/VLE)
E40D - Enviro400 (E) (ADE)
Enviro400H (ADH)
N94UD OmniDekka (SLE)
N230UD OmniCity (SP)
Trident - ALX400 (TA/TLA)

Twickenham based DPS703, one of twenty-seven 10.1m Pointers operated by London United heads away from Richmond on route 419. *Photo: Ken Carr*

Metrobus

Metrobus is another part of the Go-Ahead Group, but it is managed from a separate office. It is very active in South London. 609 pulls into Sydenham Sainsburys whilst working route 181. *Photo: Ken Carr*

Garages

C	Croydon
MB	Orpington

Fleet Total

420

Double Deckers - 152
Single Deckers - 278

PVR = 268

Head Office:
Wheatstone Close, Manor
Royal, Crawley RH10 9UA

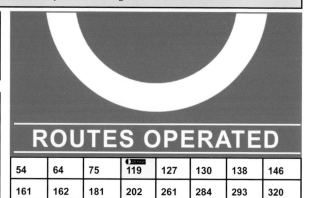

ROUTES OPERATED

54	64	75	119	127	130	138	146
161	162	181	202	261	284	293	320
336	352	353	358	359	367	405	464
612	654	B14	N64	R1	R2	R3	R4
R5	R6	R7	R8	R9	R10	R11	T32

Single Deckers Operated

Dart - Esteem
Dart - Pointer
Dart Pointer 2
E20D - Enviro200 (E)
E200 - Enviro200
MAN 12.240NL - East Lancs
MAN 14.240NL - Enviro200
MAN 14.240NL - Evolution
N94UB OmniCity
N94UB OmniTown
N230UB OmniCity

Double Deckers Operated

N94UD OmniDekka
N230UD - Olympus
N230UD OmniCity
N230UD OmniDekka

Metrobus operates more Scania N94UD OmniDekkas than any other type of double-decker. Here, 933 passes along Orpington High Street after starting its journey at the nearby Ramsden Estate. The company also operates non-TfL routes in Surrey and Sussex with buses painted in a two-tone blue livery. *Photo: Ken Carr*

Metroline

Metroline's main area of operation is North, North West & Central London, but they also operate routes to Richmond and Staines in the South-West. Most routes that visit Central London use double-deckers. However, there are a few that do not, such as this one. DE1168 started this journey at Lancaster Gate. *Photo: Peter Horrex*

Garages

AH	Brentford
W	Cricklewood
EW	Edgware
HD	Harrow Weald
HT	Holloway
KC	Kings Cross
PV	Perivale
PB	Potters Bar
PA	West Perivale
AC	Willesden

Fleet Total

1339

Double Deckers - 901
Single Deckers - 338

PVR = 927

Head Office:
Hygeia House, 66 College Road,
Harrow, Middlesex, HA1 1BE

ROUTES OPERATED

4	6 (24 hour)	7	16	17	32	43 (24 hour)	46
52	79	82	90	91	98	105 (24 hour)	107
113	134 (24 hour)	139 (24 hour)	140 (24 hour)	143	182	186	189 (24 hour)
190	204	209	210	214 (24 hour)	217	232	234
237	240	260	263	271 (24 hour)	274	297 (24 hour)	302
316	326	332	383	384	390 (24 hour)	395	460
603	606	609	611	626	635	643	C11
E2	E6	E8	H12	N5	N7	N16	N20
N52	N91	N98	N113	W7	W8	W9	

Single Deckers Operated

Dart - Pointer (DLD/DLM/DP/DSD)
Dart - Pointer 2 (DLD/DP/DSD)
E20D - Enviro200 (E) (DE/DEM)
E200Dart - Enviro200 (DE/DEL/DES)
E200Dart - Evolution (DM)
MAN 12.240 - Evolution (MM)
Optare Tempo Hybrid (OTH)

Double Deckers Operated

B7TL - President (VP/VPL)
B9TL - Eclipse Gemini 2 (VW)
B9TL - Eclipse Gemini 2 (E) (VW)
E40D - Enviro400 (E) (TE)
E40D - Enviro400H (E) (TEH)
Enviro400 (TE)
Enviro400H (TEH)
N230UD - Olympus (SEL)
Trident - ALX400 (TA/TAL)
Trident - President (TP/TPL)

Around 70% of the Metroline fleet comprises double-deckers. VPL198 a B7TL 10.6m President, turns into Station Road at Harrow. *Photo: Ken Carr*

Quality Line

A trio of Quality Line's single-deckers in Kingston. OP33 heads the queue, Mercedes-Benz Citaro MCL12 is working the recently acquired X26 and another Optare Solo, OP31 pulls in at the rear.
Photo: Jack Marian

Garages

EB   Epsom

Fleet Total

84

Double Deckers - 13
Single Deckers - 71

PVR = 72

Head Office:
Blenheim Road, Longmead Est,
Epsom, Surrey KT19 9AF

ROUTES OPERATED

404	406	411	418	463	465	467	470
641	K5	S1	S3	S4	X26		

Single Deckers Operated

Citaro (MCL)
Dart - ALX200 (SD)
Dart - Esteem (SD)
Dart - East Lancs (SD)
E200Dart - East Lancs (SD)
E200Dart - Enviro 200 (SD)
Optare Solo (OP)
Optare Versa (OV)

Double Deckers Operated

Enviro400 (DD)

Although retaining its Quality Line branding, the company is now owned by RATP who also own London Sovereign. The company operates thirteen Enviro400s for routes 406, 418 and 467. DD13 the newest Enviro400 in the fleet has been manufactured to the European Community Whole Vehicle Type Approval standard. It is about to leave the stand at Kingston. *Photo: Jack Marian*

Stagecoach

The large majority of Stagecoach's London fleet is made up of Alexander Dennis products. One of the types used that isn't is the Optare Versa. The company has fourteen of these. *Photo: Ken Carr*

Garages

BK	Barking
TB	Bromley
BW	Bow
TL	Catford
T	Leyton
PD	Plumstead
RM	Rainham
NS	Romford
WH	West Ham

Fleet Total

1344

Double Deckers - 1086
Single Deckers - 258

PVR = 1004

Head Office:
Stephenson Street, Canning
Town E16 4SA.

ROUTES OPERATED

5	8	15	15H	47	48	51	53 *24 hour*
55	56	61	62	69 *24 hour*	86	96	97
99	101	103	104	106	115	122	124
136	145	147	158	169	174	175	177
178	199	205 *24 hour*	208	215	227	230	238 *24 hour*
241	246	247	248	257	262	269	273
275	277 *24 hour*	287	291	294	296	314	323
330	354	356	366	372	380	386	387
396	469	472 *24 hour*	473	488	496	601	602
636	637	638	660	664	672	674	687
D3	N8	N15	N47	N55	N86	N136	N550
P4							

Single Deckers Operated

Citaro
Dart - ALX200
Dart - Pointer
Dart - Pointer 2
E20D - Enviro200 (E)
E200 Dart - Enviro200
Optare Tempo Hybrid
Optare Versa

Double Deckers Operated

E40D - Enviro400 (E)
E40D - Enviro400H (E)
Enviro400
N230UD OmniCity
Routemaster
Trident - ALX400

Stagecoach is using hybrid Enviro400s on Route 15. Twenty-six, including this one, 12142, are based at Bow garage for this service. It passes St Paul's Cathedral heading for Blackwall station. *Photo: Ken Carr*

Sullivan Buses

Garages

SM   South Mimms

Sullivan Buses' return to TfL operations began with the 298. Six Enviro200s were bought to run on this route. AE14 heads south through Cockfosters. This batch of Enviro200s is built to ECWVTA specification. *Photo: Ken Carr*

Fleet Total

20

Double Deckers - 14
Single Deckers - 6

PVR = 16

Head Office:
First Floor, Deards House, St Albans Road, South Mimms Service Area, EN6 3NE

ROUTES OPERATED

298	628	653	683	688			

Single Deckers Operated

E20 - Enviro 200 (E) (AE)

From the start of the new school year in September 2012, Sullivan's started operating four TfL school routes. These feature a variety of double-deckers from their interesting fleet. TN2, a Trident Lolyne awaits its next turn at South Mimms. *Photo: Ken Carr*

Double Deckers Operated

B7TL - Eclipse Gemini (WVL)
B7TL - President (VP)
B7TL - Vyking (ELV)
Trident - Lolyne (TN)
Trident - President (TPL)

www.sullivanbuses.com

TN2

306

PO51 UML

The Buses

This section looks at the different types of buses you will find on TfL routes - single-deckers first, then double-deckers. For each type we include details of builder, build dates, operators and the routes on which they can be found (those shown in *italics* are routes that they are not rostered to work but invariably do). However, this is not an exact science. Some garages vary the types they put out on some routes (or do it on all routes!), while others stick religiously to the type nominated in the contract. It goes without saying that failures and non-availability often conspire to produce other interesting workings.

Since the publication of the First Edition, several new types have appeared in the London area. New Bus for London has finally arrived, as has the Wrightbus Streetlite in both door-forward (DF) and wheel-forward (WF) configurations. In addition, Alexander Dennis now builds its Enviro 200 and Enviro 400 models to the ECWVTA (European Community Whole Vehicle Type Approval) specification. since this became the UK standard in October 2011. Wrightbus has been building double-deckers to this specification since the introduction of DW401 in April 2011. The 'whole vehicle' models are listed separately in the guide.

Older types continue to be gradually phased out of London use but the main casualty of the past twelve months has been the bendibus - completely eliminated from TfL routes by the end of 2011.

When an operator orders a new bus, there are numerous choices to make - what type of chassis, with which engine, what type of axles, which body, seat configuration, style of décor, to name but a few. Some manufacturers offer ready-made packages but it is perfectly possible to create a fully custom bus. If you've ever ordered a new car from scratch, rather than buying a vehicle already in the dealer's stock, you'll understand how this process works.

Some manufacturers, such as Alexander Dennis Ltd, produce chassis and body. They can either be supplied together (often referred to as an 'integral bus') or the body can be fitted to a chassis built by another maker (and, in ADL's case, *vice versa*). Others concentrate on one or the other. Volvo and VDL (which includes the bus division of the former DAF) produce only chassis. Wrightbus concentrates on bodywork, but now offers what it calls an integral bus even though the chassis components are supplied by VDL.

Optare has been able to supply both chassis and body for single-deckers for the past two years, following the acquisition of East Lancs Coachbuilders but, until now, has relied on other manufacturers' chassis to power its double-deck bodies. At present, the company will only take double-deck orders for niche markets, like open-top sight-seeing buses, but we are still waiting to see if plans to launch its own complete double-deck product (with a Mercedes-Benz engine), will come to fruition.

Scania's latest double-deck offering is an integral bus built in Poland – the OmniCity.

In broad terms, there are only four, or possibly five, double-deck models currently available new to TfL operators:

Alexander Dennis Enviro400 (straight diesel or diesel-electric hybrid)

Volvo B9TL/Wrightbus Eclipse Gemini 2 (straight diesel) or Volvo B5LH/Wrightbus Gemini 2 (diesel-electric)

Scania OmniCity CN230UD integral (straight diesel only)

Wrightbus Gemini 2 DL integral (only taken up by Arriva in quantity)

Wrightbus New Bus for London (diesel-electric)

Of all these suppliers, Alexander Dennis has the greatest presence, thanks to the ubiquitous Enviro200 single-decker and the highly-successful Enviro400. However, competition is fierce: The combination of Volvo B9TL chassis and Wrightbus Gemini 2 body has generated significant orders from TfL operators since 2009 and Volvo has ambitious plans to insert its B9 chassis under a new MCV double-deck body to be built in Egypt (see below). In the single-deck market, Wrightbus, Optare and Mercedes are striving to challenge ADL's dominance.

The Volvo/MCV double-deck project is equally interesting but for different reasons. A prototype, VM1, is currently being evaluated by Go-Ahead in east London, mostly on Route 425 or 474. Like the first attempt to introduce a similar model, weight continues to be an issue. London Buses' specification calls for a double-decker to carry 87 passengers, either seated or standing. To calculate an accurate laden weight for each bus type, a nominal figure is assigned to each passenger. This has recently been increased from 63.5kg (10 stone) to 68kg (10 stone 10 lbs) per person, which is bad timing for Volvo/MCV. The latest prototype was already overweight, so the bus had to be given special dispensation to operate in London, with its maximum permitted load reduced to 82 passengers. How effectively this problem is addressed will decide whether the type enters service in London in any numbers.

While we're on physical requirements, London Buses also insists that double-deckers have two sets of doors (and most single-deckers), top deck climate control, fire suppression systems and environmentally-friendly exhaust traps. The constant requirement to reduce emissions has enforced tougher and tougher restrictions on builders and operators and yet another new European standard – known as Euro 6 – will soon be applied to new orders.

Obviously, not everything running in the capital is brand-new. Numerous older types can be found, particularly Dennis chassis single-deckers with a host of different bodies. Double-deckers with Dennis, Volvo and DAF chassis remain in abundance, especially with ALX400 and President bodies, and many enthusiasts find these by far the most interesting members of the London fleet. You can even find a rapidly dwindling number of Plaxton Presidents with centre staircases! And for connoisseurs of the exotic, another unique trio can be found most days on route 85 – the VE class with Enviro400 bodies on Volvo B9TL chassis. These are unique in London and possibly everywhere else.

London is gradually gaining more hybrid buses. Initially, all of them were subsidised by Government grant - the so-called Green Fund. Round One covered 100% of the extra cost of hybrid technology, Round Two met 90% of it. Round Three, announced in March 2012, will cover 80% of the extra cost of 70 more hybrid buses but, as we go to press, there has been no announcement of which operators will benefit and which models (and routes) will be involved.

In the hiatus between Rounds Two and Three, some operators met the extra cost themselves, perhaps because they felt the potential fuel savings were worth the investment. Whatever the reasoning, there are currently some 300 hybrids (plus the gas buses) running in London and a further 150 are expected by April 2013. Time will tell if the Mayor's 'pledge' to introduced 600 extra NBfL hybrids materialises by the aspirational date of 2016. At least progress generally is much more rapid now than the rather pitiful figure of 108 hybrids introduced between 2006 and 2011 but, with more than 8,000 buses in the London fleets, 100% 'low carbon' remains a long way off.

Hybrid technology has slowly been introduced onto TfL services, with just over 300 now operating on London's streets. Boris Johnson's pledge to order 600 of Wrightbus's New Bus For London would drastically alter the percentages, but only time will tell if this becomes a reality. *Photo: Chris Fleetwood*

Single-Deckers

B6BLE - Crusader2 10.2m

These can be a little tricky to find. Although nominally allocated to H18 & H19 they sometimes appear on other London routes and non-TfL routes operated by Arriva The Shires. *Photo: David McKay*

Built by: **Dennis/Alexander**   Introduced: **1999**   Number: **3**
Operators (routes): **Arriva The Shires (H18, H19)**

Citaro 12m

The number of these Citaros is gradually increasing, both Quality Line & Stagecoach have recently introduced them to their fleets. *Photo: Jack Marian*

Built: **Mercedes-Benz**   Introduced: **2009, 2011 & 2012**   Number: **77**
Operators (routes): **Go-Ahead (507, 521), London United (203), Quality Line (X26) Stagecoach (227)**

Dart - ALX200 8.9m

A handful of the ALX200s are hanging on in London. Quality Line's Epsom garage plays host to three out of the four operated by the company. *Photo: Ken Carr*

Built by: **Dennis/Alexander**   Introduced: **2000 & 2001**   Number: **16**
Operators (routes): **Quality Line (S3), Stagecoach (273, 380)**

Dart - Capital 8.9m

The Dart Capital is another type that is disappearing fast from TfL work. This one for example, Metrobus 148 shown loading-up at New Addington is no longer used on TfL work. *Photo: Jack Marian*

Built by: **Dennis/Marshall, TransBus/Marshall**   Introduced: **1999-2002**   Number: **13**
Operators (routes): **First (193), Go-Ahead (W10)**

Dart - Capital 10.2m

DML41377 has been replaced on the 224 by new Enviro200s and is no longer used in London. First's only remaining 10.2m Capitals work out of Dagenham. *Photo: Jack Marian*

Built by: **Dennis/Marshall**   Introduced: **1998-2001**   Number: **5**
Operators (routes): **First (646, 953)**

Dart - Esteem 9.0m

Metrobus is the only operator of the Dart with the East Lancs Esteem body. *Photo: Robert Mighton*

Built by: **Alexander Dennis/East Lancs**   Introduced: **2006**   Number: **21**
Operators (routes): **Metrobus (138, 146, 336, 367)**

Dart - Evolution 9.2m

These can normally be found on route W19. However, on this occassion ED10 was being readied at Rainham garage for use on a shuttle service being operated for participants in the Olympic Games opening ceremony rehearsals. *Photo: Ken Carr*

Built by: **Alexander Dennis/MCV**   Introduced: **2006**   Number: **9**
Operators (routes): **Go-Ahead (W19)**

Dart - Evolution 10.8m

Go-Ahead also has eight of the longer version Evolutions. Here, ED5 is on the stand at Canning Town. They have been replaced by Enviro200s on route 300 and can now be found on the 108 & 129. *Photo: Jack Marian*

Built by: **Alexander Dennis/MCV**   Introduced: **2006**   Number: **8**
Operators (routes): **Go-Ahead (108, 129)**

Dart - Myllennium 9m

Only five of this type work in London. All are operated by Quality Line and can normally be found on the S3, like SD39 which stops to pick-up in Sutton. *Photo: Adam Murray*

Built by: **Alexander Dennis/East Lancs**   Introduced: **2005**   Number: **5**
Operators (routes): **Quality Line (*463*, S3)**

Dart - Nimbus 8.9m

The nine single-door Caetano Nimbus operated by CT Plus are the only ones of this type in London. DCS6 manoeuvres onto the stand at Homerton hospital. Photo: *Photo: Ken Carr*

Built by: **TransBus/Caetano**   Introduced: **2002 & 2003**   Number: **9**
Operators (routes): **CT Plus (394)**

Dart - Nimbus 10.5m

More numerous is the longer two-door version. Prior to losing this route to Go-Ahead in September 2011, DMC41512 is seen on the stand at Crossharbour. *Photo: Jack Marian.*

Built by: **Dennis/Caetano, TransBus/Caetano, Alexander Dennis/Caetano**
Introduced: **2001-04**   Number: **83**
Operators (routes): **Abellio (112, 455, H25, U7), CT Plus (153), First (*U1*, U2, U3 *U5*, *U10*)**

Dart - Nimbus 11.0m

Abellio has a fleet of twelve 11m Dart Nimbus. 8748 is on its regular route at Brentford. *Photo: Ken Carr*

Built by: **TransBus/Caetano**   Introduced: **2003**   Number: **12**
Operators (routes): **Abellio (235)**

Dart - Pointer 8.8m

These small Dart Pointers are gradually being replaced. PDL74 waits at Chingford station, but it and its classmates were replaced on this service in June 2012. *Photo: Jack Marian*

Built by: **Dennis/Plaxton, Dennis/Alexander, TransBus, Alexander Dennis**
Introduced: **2000/2002 - 2006**   Number: **119**
Operators (routes): **Abellio (322, *481*, H20, P13, U9), Arriva (318, 327, 377, 382, W16), CT Plus (385), Go-Ahead (201, 315, 424, G1), Metrobus (352, 464, *R1*, R3, R4, R5, R6, R7), Stagecoach (380)**

Dart - Pointer 9.3m

PDL99 takes a breather at the Crystal Palace bus station. *Photo: Jack Marian*

Built by: **TransBus, Alexander Dennis**   Introduced: **2002/03/06**   Number: **53**
Operators (routes): **Arriva (*444*, 410, 450, W6), Arriva Southern Counties (346), Metroline (W9), Stagecoach (291, *386*)**

Dart - Pointer 10.1m

A number of operators still use the 10.1m Pointer. Amongst them is Arriva The Shires, The company's 3804 stands at Harrow-on-the-Hill bus station. *Photo: Ken Carr*

Built by: **Dennis/Plaxton, TransBus, Alexander Dennis**   Introduced: **2000/2002 & 2003**   Number: **119**
Operators (routes): **Abellio (152, U7), Arriva (*166*, 312, T31), Arriva The Shires (H18, H19) Go-Ahead (164, 201, 219, 225, 355, 485), London Sovereign (398), London United (*371*), Stagecoach (178, P4)**

Dart - Pointer 10.7m

215 pulls away from New Addington Interchange. *Photo: Robert Mighton*

Built by: **TransBus**   Introduced: **2003 & 2004**   Number: **15**
Operators (routes): **Go-Ahead (170), Metrobus (130)**

Dart - Pointer 2 8.8m

This service connects the Tesco at Hayes to the one at Osterley. *Photo: Jack Marion*

Built by: **Dennis/Plaxton**   Introduced: **2000 & 2001**   Number: **14**
Operators (routes): **Abellio (*H28*), London United (K4)**

Dart - Pointer 2 9.3m

Whenever you wander around the City of London, you seem to constantly come across route 100. 8310 runs alongside St Paul's Cathedral on St Paul's Church Yard. *Photo: Ken Carr*

Built by: **Dennis/Plaxton, Alexander Dennis**   Introduced: **1999/01/04/05**   Number: **11**
Operators (routes): **Abellio (100)**

Dart - Pointer 2 10.1m

DPS595 is about two-thirds into its journey from Fulwell on route 33 as it passes through Sheen. *Photo: Ken Carr*

Built by: **Dennis/Plaxton, TransBus, Alexander Dennis**   Introduced: **1997-2004/06**   Number: **171**
Operators (routes): **Abellio (152), London Sovereign (H9, H10, *H11*, H13, *H14*, H17), London United (33, 110, 116, 216, 265, 419, H22, *H37*, K2, K3), Metroline (46, 214, *C11*)**

Dart - Pointer 2 10.7m

Metrobus uses the long Pointer 2s on this route. 328 pauses at New Addington. *Photo: Jack Marian*

Built by: **Dennis/Plaxton, Alexander Dennis**   Introduced: **1998-2000/06**   Number: **71**
Operators (routes): **Arriva (***255***), Arriva Kent Thameside (126), London United (222), Metrobus (130)**

E20D - Enviro200 8.9m

Enviro200s are now being built to the ECWVTA standard and the chassis is now designated E20D rather than Dart 4. One of the first to be built was Metrobus's 174 which is allocated to Orpington. *Photo: David McKay*

Built: **Alexander Dennis**   Introduced:**2011-2012**   Number: **29**
Operators (routes): **Arriva (379), Metrobus (R1, R4, R11), Stagecoach (124)**

E20D - Enviro200 9.6m

When the ECWVTA standard was introduced, the 9.3 metre Enviro 200 was adjusted to 9.6 metre length. First's DM44203 arrives in Harrow on route 223. *Photo: Jack Marian*

Built: **Alexander Dennis**   Introduced: **2011-2012**   Number: **64**
Operators (routes): **Arriva (397, W11), First (223, W14), Go-Ahead (W16), Metroline (234, W9)**

E20D - Enviro200 10.2m

The ECWVTA buses can be easily recognised by the four amber marker lights along the lower bodysides, as displayed by SE156 at Surrey Quays. *Photo: Jack Marian*

Built: **Alexander Dennis**   Introduced: **2011-2012**   Number: **125**
Operators (routes): **Abellio (290), First (70, 224, W15), Go-Ahead (413, 493, D8, P12), Metroline (90), Stagecoach (314), Sullivans (298)**

E20D - Enviro200 10.8m

In June 2012, Arriva introduced 10.8m versions of the new style Enviro onto this route. *Photo: Dave McKay*

Built: **Alexander Dennis** Introduced: **2011-2012** Number: **46**
Operators (routes): **Abellio (490), Arriva (289, 313) First (206, 236, 308),**

E200Dart - Enviro200 8.9m

Stagecoach has twenty-one of the short Enviro200 built to the old spec. 36323 pulls away from the stop outside Sainsbury's in Sydenham. *Photo: Mark Jiggins*

Built: **Alexander Dennis** Introduced: **2006-11** Number: **159**
Operators (routes): **Abellio (434, 481, *H20*, H26), Arriva (192), Arriva Southern Counties (233), CT Plus (394), First (E5, E10), Go-Ahead (W4), London Sovereign (324), London United (E11, K1), Metrobus (162, B14), Metroline (383, 384, W9), Quality lIne (S3), Stagecoach (273, 354, 356)**

E200Dart - Enviro200 9.3m

Go-Ahead acquired eight of the 9.3 metre length E200 when it bought out the Northumberland Park operation from First Capital and renumbered them in this SEN series.

Built: Alexander Dennis   Introduced: **2007-2011**   Number: **68**
Operators (routes): **Abellio (100, 484), Arriva (393), First (339), Go-Ahead (299, 389, 399, P5), Stagecoach (*291*, 386)**

E200Dart - Enviro200 10.2m

The most numerous single-deck type in London, these can be found working for virtually all operators. London Sovereign's DE92 picks up in Kenton. *Photo: Ken Carr*

Built: Alexander Dennis   Introduced: **2007-2011**   Number: **704**
Operators (routes): **Abellio (117, 152, 407, C10, R68, R70), Arriva (166, 173, 184, *312*, 325, 491, T31), Arriva Southern Counties (B12, *370*, 375, 499), First (95, 165, 187, 195, 226, 228, 245, 331, 368, 487, 498, A10, E7, E9, RV1, U1, *U2, U3*, U5, U10, W15), Go-Ahead (200, 244, 300, B11, B16), London Sovereign (251, 398, H9, H10, H11, H13, H14, H17), London United (33, 72, *216*, 272, 285, 371, 440, C1), Metrobus (R9), Metroline (143, 209, 232, 274, 316, 326, 395, C11, E8), Stagecoach (62, 296, 323, 366, 469, 488, D3)**

E200Dart - Enviro200 10.8m

Go-Ahead's SE27 is receiving a battery change in the yard at Rainham. *Photo: Ken Carr*

Built: **Alexander Dennis**   Introduced: **2007-2011**   Number: **124**
Operators (routes): **Abellio (T33), Arriva Southern Counties (66, 256, 286, 428), Go-Ahead (170, 276, 347, 362, 364, 376, D6), London United (423, H98), Metroline, Stagecoach (246, 372)**

E200Dart - Enviro200H 10.2m

The five hybrid Enviro200s operate out of Fulwell usually on route 371. *Photo: Ken Carr*

Built: **Alexander Dennis**   Introduced: **2009**   Number: **5**
Operators (routes): **London United (371)**

E200Dart - Esteem 9.4m

CT Plus has six of these Darts with East Lancs Esteem bodywork and normally puts them out on route W13.
Photo: Robert Mighton

Built: **Alexander Dennis/East Lancs**　　　Introduced: **2007**　　　Number: **6**
Operators (routes): **CT Plus (W13)**

E200Dart - Esteem 9.5m

Quality Line tends to use these on their routes operating around Sutton. SD48 picks-up in Manor Road,
Sutton whilst working to the Marks & Spencer at Banstead. *Photo: Adam Murray*

Built: Alexander **Dennis/East Lancs**　　　Introduced: **2007**　　　Number: **9**
Operators (routes): **Quality Line (S1, S4)**

E200Dart - Esteem 10.4m

SOE36 waits on the bus stand adjacent to its home garage at Sutton. *Photo: Ken Carr*

Built: **Alexander Dennis/Optare**   Introduced: **2009**   Number: **40**
Operators (routes): **Go-Ahead (163, 164, *200*, *219*, *413*)**

E200Dart - Evolution 10.4m

Metroline's Evolutions tend to work on route 190, but you can often find one on the E8. *Photo: Jack Marian*

Built: **Alexander Dennis/MCV**   Introduced: **2009**   Number: **21**
Operators (routes): **Go-Ahead (190, 549), Metroline (*E8*, 190)**

Electrocity 10.3m

Abellio's five Electrocitys share route R70 with Enviro200s. Photo: Jack Marian

Built: **Wrightbus**   Introduced: **2007/08/11**   Number: **12**
Operators (routes): **Abellio (R70), Go-Ahead (360)**

Electrocity 10.4m

Go-Ahead also operate a slightly longer version of the Electrocity on route 360. All are based at Camberwell
Photo: Rhys Mccollin-Johnson

Built: **Wrightbus**   Introduced: **2005 & 2006**   Number: **6**
Operators (routes): **Go-Ahead (360)**

MAN 12.240 - Evolution 10.4m

MM776 arrives at Brent Cross shopping centre. *Photo: Robert Mighton*

Built: **MAN/MCV**   Introduced: **2007**   Number: **38**
Operators (routes): **Metroline (90, E6)**

MAN 12.240NL - East Lancs 10.3m

Metrobus have five of these based at Orpington for use on the R2. *Photo: Ken Carr*

Built: **MAN/East Lancs**   Introduced: **2007**   Number: **5**
Operators (routes): **Metrobus (R2)**

MAN 14.240NL - Enviro200 10.7m

Only three Enviro200s on MAN chassis operate on TfL routes, all three operating from Metrobus' Croydon garage. *Photo: Jack Marian*

Built: **MAN/Alexander Dennis** Introduced: **2008** Number: **3**
Operators (routes): **Metrobus (359, T32)**

MAN 14.240NL - Evolution 10.8m

Yet another type unique to Metrobus. All fifteen are based at Croydon for use on the 202. *Photo: Mark Jiggins*

Built: **MAN/MCV** Introduced: **2009** Number: **15**
Operators (routes): **Metrobus (202)**

N94UB - East Lancs 10.6m

ELS7 is on the approach to Tower Bridge, all fourteen of these are based at Camberwell. *Photo: Peter Horrex*

Built: **Scania/East Lancs**   Introduced: **2002**   Number: **14**
Operators (routes): **Go-Ahead (42)**

N94UB - Esteem 10.6m

Another unique type operated by Metrobus, all are based at Orpington. *Photo Jack Marian*

Built: **Scania/East Lancs**   Introduced: **2006**   Number: **23**
Operators (routes): **Metrobus (181, 284)**

N94UB OmniCity 12m

At Crystal Palace, the driver of 518 prepares to take his bus back to Kent. *Photo: Jack Marian*

Built: **Scania**   Introduced: **2002-2005**   Number: **46**
Operators (routes): **Metrobus (358)**

N230UB OmniCity 12m

Metrobus deployed these 12 metre Scanias on the X26 until it lost the route to Quality Line. They're most likely to be on the 293 now, but they do stray onto other routes. *Photo: Adam Murray*

Built: **Scania**   Introduced: **2007-09**   Number: **23**
Operators (routes): **Metrobus (293)**

SB120 - Cadet 9.4m

Arriva have eighteen of these based at Thornton Heath for use on the 410. *Photo: Jack Marian*

Built: **DAF/Wrightbus**   Introduced: **2003 & 2004**   Number: **42**
Operators (routes): **Arriva (410), Arriva Southern Counties (428, B13, B15), Go-Ahead (132, 201)**

SB120 - Cadet 10.2m

The mid-length Cadet is only used by Arriva and its constituent companies. *Photo: Ken Carr*

Built: **DAF/Wrightbus, VDL/Wrightbus**   Introduced: **2001-2003/06**   Number: **84**
Operators (routes): **Arriva (255, 444), Arriva Southern Counties (499), Arriva the Shires (268, 288, 303, 305, H18, H19)**

SB120 - Cadet 10.8m

Go-Ahead's SB120 Cadet is known as the Volvo Merit for some unexplained reason. An allocation of twenty-five is split between Bexleyheath and New Cross garages. *Photo: Robert Mighton*

Built: **DAF/Wrightbus, VDL/Wrightbus**   Introduced: **2002 & 2004**   Number: **31**
Operators (routes): **Arriva (313), Go-Ahead (108, 132)**

SB200 - Pulsar 2 (Hydrogen Fuel Cell) 11.9m

All five hydrogen buses are based at First's Lea Interchange garage where a special fuelling point has been installed. When they work, they appear on route RV1. *Photo: Peter Horrex*

Built: **VDL/Wrightbus**   Introduced: **2010 & 2011**   Number: **5**
Operators (routes): **First (RV1)**

Solo 7.8m

Routes H2 & H3 are circular routes around the Golders Green area. Both are operated by 7.8m Optare Solos. 2470 pulls away from the dedicated bus stop at Golders Green. *Photo: Ken Carr*

Built: **Optare**   Introduced: **2006 & 2007**   Number: **6**
Operators (routes): **Arriva the Shires (H2, H3)**

Solo 8.5m

OP16 pulls away from the Reigate Avenue stop in Rosehill. *Photo: Adam Murray*

Built: **Optare**   Introduced: **2001-2003**   Number: **21**
Operators (routes): **Quality Line (404, 470)**

Solo 8.8m

OP23 will shortly leave Quality Line's Epsom garage for another stint on the 463. *Photo: Ken Carr*

Built: **Optare**   Introduced: **2009 & 2011**   Number: **18**
Operators (routes): **CT Plus (W5), Quality Line (463, K5)**

Solo 9.6m

The newest Solos in London are the 9.6m two-door versions used by CT Plus on the 309. *Photo David McKay*

Built: **Optare**   Introduced: **2012**   Number: **9**
Operators (routes): **CT Plus (309)**

Solo SE 7.1m

The smallest buses in London are Metrobus pair 101 and 102. *Photo: Robert Mighton*

Built: **Optare**   Introduced: **2006**   Number: **2**
Operators (routes): **Metrobus (R8)**

Solo SE 7.8m

OS5 calls in at South Woodford station whilst working route W12. *Photo: Jack Marian*

Built: **Optare**   Introduced: **2010**   Number: **7**
Operators (routes): **CT Plus (W12)**

StreetLite DF - 10.4m

First is operating a solitary door-forward Streetlite, WM47400. It is based at Willesden Junction and is normally put to work on route 228. *Photo: Jack Marian*

Built: **Wrightbus**   Introduced: **2011**   Number: **1**
Operators (routes): **First (228)**

StreetLite WF - 8.8m

The rather strange looking wheel forward StreetLite has been ordered by Go-Ahead. Nine have been delivered to Rainham garage for use on the 462. *Photo: Peter Horrex*

Built: **Wrightbus**   Introduced: **2012**   Number: **9**
Operators (routes): **Go-Ahead (462)**

Tempo 12.0m

All sixteen of London United's Optare Tempos are allocated to Hounslow garage, normally to be found on the H37, such as OT3 coming to the end of its run to Richmond Manor Circus. *Photo: Ken Carr*

Built: **Optare**   Introduced: **2011**   Number: **16**
Operators (routes): **London United (H37)**

Tempo Hybrid 10.6m

OTH975, one of five hybrid Tempos operated by Metroline from Brentford garage. *Photo: Jack Marian*

Built: **Optare**   Introduced: **2008 & 2009**   Number: **10**
Operators (routes): **Metroline (E8), Stagecoach (380)**

Versa 10.4m

25307 stands inside Plumstead garage shortly before its transfer north of the river to Barking garage at the beginning of April 2012. *Photo: Ken Carr*

Built: **Optare**   Introduced **2008 & 09**   Number: **50**
Operators (routes): **London United (283, 391), Stagecoach (62, 396)**

Versa 11.1m

Quality Line has eight of the longer Versa. OV03 arrives at Kingston on its regular route 411. *Photo: Jack Marian*

Built: **Optare** Introduced: **2010** Number: **8**
Operators (routes): **Quality Line (411, 465)**

Versa Hybrid 10.4m

Optare's Versa Hybrid, HOV1 is currently operating out of Go-Ahead's Camberwell garage and when in use can usually be found on route 360. *Photo: Mark Leonard*

Built: **Optare** Introduced: **2007** Number: **1**
Operators (routes): **Go-Ahead (360)**

Double-Deckers

B5LH - Eclipse Gemini 2 10.4m

The first sixteen of Go-Ahead's Volvo hybrids are based at Camberwell for route 12.. *Photo: Robert Mighton*

Built: **Volvo/Wrightbus**   Introduced: **2009-2011**   Number: **62**
Operators (routes): **Arriva (73, 76, 149, 243), Go-Ahead (12)**

B5LH - Eclipse Gemini 2 10.5m

WHV17-31 are built to ECWVTA spec and are ten centimetres longer. This batch is allocated to Stockwell for route 19. *Photo: David McKay*

Built: **Volvo/Wrightbus**   Introduced: **2012**   Number: **25**
Operators (routes): **Go-Ahead (19)**

Buses with the Volvo B7TL chassis are quite popular with enthusiasts. If you get a good one it can be very noisy! 6109 was formerly VLA109 and has recently been transferred from Arriva to Arriva The Shires.
Photo: Ken Carr

Built: **Volvo/Alexander, Volvo/TransBus**   Introduced: **2000/02/03**   Number: **160**
Operators (routes): **Arriva** (*41*, **123, 128, 159, 415, 432**), **Arriva The Shires (340), London United** (*49, 111, 120,* **148, 220,** *H32*)

B7TL - ALX400 10.6m

One of Arriva's longer Volvo-powered ALX400s, Norwood based VLA55, picks-up passengers at Neathouse Place in Victoria. *Photo: Ken Carr*

Built: **Volvo/TransBus, Volvo/Alexander Dennis**   Introduced: **2003-2005**   Number: **73**
Operators (routes): **Arriva (2, 176, 415)**

B7TL - Eclipse Gemini 10.1m

The Volvo chassis is also underneath Eclipse Geminis. Stockwell's WVL133 runs along Aldwych on a route it shares with B7TL Presidents. *Photo: Ken Carr*

Built: **Volvo/Wrightbus**   Introduced: **2001-2005**   Number: **529**
Operators (routes): **Arriva (*29*, 141, *144*, 168, 221, 242, 253, 254, *279*, 349), First (28, 31, *83*, 328, 607), Go-Ahead (11, 14, 22, 44, *45*, 68, 74, 77, 85, 87, *118*, 155, 270, 333, 430, X68)**

B7TL - Eclipse Gemini 10.6m

VWL34, based at Mandela Way, runs along Aldwych. *Photo: Ken Carr*

Built: **Volvo/Wrightbus**   Introduced: **2002-2006**   Number: **155**
Operators (routes): **Abellio (157, 188, 343, 381), Arriva (253, 254), First (28, *31*, 92), Go-Ahead (1, 180, 185)**

B7TL - Myllennium Vyking 10.4m

VE3 splashes through the rain. Ten of these are operated by London United and based at Shepherd's Bush to work route 49. *Photo: David McKay*

Built: **Volvo/East Lancs**   Introduced: **2002 & 2004**   Number: **10**
Operators (routes): **London United (49)**

B7TL - Myllennium Vyking 11.0m

The longer version is operated by both London Sovereign & London United. The latter has thirty-two and all are based at Stamford Brook. *Photo: Ken Carr*

Built: **Volvo/East Lancs**   Introduced: **2004**   Number: **45**
Operators (routes): **London Sovereign (*13*, 114, *183*, *292*), London United (9, 27)**

B7TL - President 10.0m

There are still plenty of these Presidents in service, but they are gradually being replaced by newer buses. VP614 from Harrow Weald garage heads away from Harrow on route 140. *Photo: Ken Carr*

Built: **Volvo/Plaxton, Volvo/TransBus, Volvo/Alexander Dennis**
Introduced: **2000-2005**   Number: **450**
Operators (routes): **Go-Ahead (36, 44, 45, 63, *68*, 77, 87, 88, *89*, *93*, *118*, *151*, *154*, 155, *171*, 185, 200, 213, 270, 321, 333, 363, 401, 468, X68), London United (*120*, H32), Metroline (*4*, 6, *17*, *43*, 98, *134*, 140, 182, 260, 271, 302, 460, H12)**

VPL218, is one of the dwindling number of the 10.6m variant. It is based at Edgware and is a regular on route 240. *Photo: Ken Carr*

Built: **Volvo/Plaxton, Volvo/TransBus, Volvo/Alexander Dennis**
Introduced: **2000-2005**   Number: **169**
Operators (routes): **Go-Ahead (67, *259*, *476*), London Sovereign (*13*, *114*, *183*, 292), Metroline (*4*, 43, 52, 107, 113, *134*, *140*, *182*, *186*, 240, 390)**

B9TL - Eclipse Gemini 2 10.4m

The Wrightbus Eclipse Gemini 2 is mounted on a third party chassis like the 'straight diesel' Volvo B9TL. Alperton's VN37793 arrives at journey's end. *Photo: Ken Carr*

Built: **Volvo/Wrightbus**   Introduced: **2009-2011**   Number: **487**
Operators (routes): **First (18, 25, 58, 83, 295, 427)**, **Go-Ahead (12, 21, *37*, 63, 171, 229, 259, 357, *363*, 401, 422, *425*, 474, 476, D7, EL1, EL2)**, **Metroline (237, 297, E2)**

B9TL - Eclipse Gemini 2 (E) 10.5m

Volvo-powered diesel buses built to ECWVTA spec are also 10 centimetres longer. Rainham's WVL462 passes through Loughton. *Photo: Peter Horrex*

Built: **Volvo/Wrightbus**   Introduced: **2012**   Number: **171**
Operators (routes): **First (266)**, **Go-Ahead (19, 20, 249)**, **Metroline (43, 79, 105, 134, W7)**

B9TL - Enviro400 10.4m

VE1 is one of three Volvo B9TL/Enviro400 combinations in London that are operated by Go-Ahead from Putney garage on route 85. *Photo: Robert Mighton*

Built: **Volvo/Alexander Dennis**   Introduced: **2008**   Number: **3**
Operators (routes): **Go-Ahead (85)**

B9TL - MCV 10.3m

VM1 in the yard at Silvertown garage. This bus is currently being trialled by Go-Ahead. *Photo: Ken Carr*

Built: **Volvo/MCV**   Introduced: **2011**   Number: **1**
Operators (routes): **Go-Ahead (474)**

CN94UD OmniCity 10.7m

London United has 186 Scania OmniCitys but only fifteen are the shorter CN94UD variant. All are based at Hounslow garage. *Photo: Jack Marian*

Built: **Scania**   Introduced: **2006**   Number: **15**
Operators (routes): **London United (120)**

DB250LF - ALX400 10.2m

The DAF chassis has only proved popular with the Arriva group of companies and has been used with a number of bodies. DLA359 has an ALX400 body and is based at Lea Valley. *Photo: Peter Horrex*

Built: **DAF/Alexander, DAF/TransBus**   Introduced: **1999-2003**   Number: **289**
Operators (routes): **Arriva (34, 41, *50*, *59*, 60, *76*, 109, *123*, 141, 176, *194*, 198, 243, 250, 253, *254*, 317, 319, *412*, 415, 417, 432, *466*), Arriva Southern Counties (370), Arriva The Shires (142, 340)**

DB250LF - ALX400 10.6m

DLA123 one of the the longer, 10.6m, DAF ALX400s, approaches its destination at Enfield. *Photo: Peter Horrex*

Built: **DAF/Alexander**   Introduced: **1998 & 1999**   Number: **55**
Operators (routes): **Arriva (121, *198*, *221*, *250*, *349*)**

DB250LF - President 10.2m

President bodied DLP86 heads along Barnet High Street. This one is based at Enfield. *Photo: Jack Marion*

Built: **DAF/TransBus**   Introduced: **2002**   Number: **35**
Operators (routes): **Arriva (34, 125, 307, 329, *349*)**

DB250LF - President 10.6m

Although based at Wood Green, DLP72 makes an unusual appearance on this Palmers Green route at Brent Cross shopping centre. *Photo: Jack Marion*

Built: **DAF/Plaxton**   Introduced: **1999 & 2001**   Number: **26**
Operators (routes): **Arriva (221)**

DB250LF - Pulsar Gemini 10.3m

Wrightbus double-deckers built onto early DAF/VDL chassis were known as Pulsar Geminis. The term Pulsar ceased to be used when the later VDL/Wright integral bus, the Gemini 2DL, was introduced. *Photo: Jack Marion*

Built: **DAF/Wrightbus, VDL/Wrightbus**   Introduced: **2003-2006**   Number: **151**
Operators (routes): **Arriva (50, 59, *60*, 137, 194, 197, 264, 403, 412, *466*), Arriva Southern Counties (492), Arriva The Shires (258)**

Over 350 of the ECWVTA specification Enviro400 have already been delivered. Arriva Southern Counties took delivery of thirteen during Winter 2011/12. Allocated to Dartford they work the 160. Here, 6465 passes through Chislehurst. Incidentally, Abellio have been trialling the first Enviro400 (9544) to be built to Euro-6 standard, it is 10cm longer than these Euro-5 buses. *Photo: Madeleine Carr*

Built: Alexander Dennis Introduced: **2011/2012** Number: **353**
Operators (routes): **Abellio (3, 211, C2), Arriva (*29*, *141*,144, 279, W3), Arriva Southern Counties (160, *492*), Go-Ahead (89, 280), London United (81, 120, 222), Metroline (32), Quality Line (406, 418, 467), Stagecoach (101,104, 136, 158, 238)**

E40D - Enviro400H (E) 10.2m

The hybrid version of the Enviro400 is also now manufactured to the ECWVTA standard. Battersea's 2415 turns from Haymarket into Pall Mall on route 3. *Photo: Ken Carr*

Built: **Alexander Dennis**   Introduced: **2005 & 2006**   Number: **132**
Operators (routes): **Abellio (3, 188, 211), First (23), Go-Ahead (436), Metroline (139, *189*),Stagecoach (15)**

Enviro400 10.1m

More than 1,000 Enviro 400s built to the former UK spec were delivered to London operators before ECWVTA became the new standard.This model is the most numerous double-decker on London streets. *Photo: Ken Carr*

Built: **Alexander Dennis**   Introduced: **2005-2011**   Number: **1105**
Operators (routes): **Abellio (35, 40, 156, *172*, *343*, 344, 414, 452), Arriva (2, 34, 50, 78, 102, *109*, 133, 135, 150, 168, 198, *242*, 250, 329, 341, 466), First (26, 30, *92*, 179, 252, *282*, 607, E1, E3), Go-Ahead (24, 36, 37, *44*, *63*, 88, *93*, 118, 196, 213, 229, 231, *270*, *333*, 337, 345, *363*, 422, 453, 486), Metroline (4, 16, 91, *113*, 139, 186, 189, 204, 210, 263, 332), Quality Line (406, 418, 467), Stagecoach (*5*, 53, 61, 62, 99, 145, 169, 174, 199, 287, 372, 387, 496)**

Enviro400 10.8m

Apart from Stagecoach's *Spirit of London* working out of West Ham, the only place to see 10.8 metre Enviro400s in the London area is on Bromley garage's route 61. *Photo: Ken Carr*

Built: **Alexander Dennis** Introduced: **2005 & 2006** Number: **11**
Operators (routes): **Stagecoach (15, 61)**

Enviro400H 10.1m

Metroline's hybrid, TEH919 awaits its next turn at its home garage of Cricklewood. *Photo: Peter Horrex*

Built: **Alexander Dennis** Introduced: **2008-2010** Number: **42**
Operators (routes): **Go-Ahead (24), London United (94, 482), Metroline (16)**

Gemini 2 DL 10.4m

Wrightbus call these "integral" buses. The chassis comprises parts supplied by VDL and is often referred to as DB300. DW301 sits on the stand outside the Hole In The Wall pub at Waterloo. *Photo: Ken Carr*

Built: **Wrightbus**   Introduced: **2009-2011**   Number: **143**
Operators (routes): **Arriva (38, 59, *76*, *123*, 137, 149, 159, 242, *243*), Arriva the Shires (*340*), First (*23*, *295*), Go-Ahead (88)**

Gemini 2 DL (E) 10.4m

Only Arriva has ordered the Gemini integral bus in quantity. This is the latest version built to ECWVTA spec. *Photo: Jack Marian*

Built: **Wrightbus (to ECWVTA spec)**   Introduced: **2011**   Number: **98**
Operators (routes): **Arriva (29, 38, 73, 242, 243)**

Gemini 2 HEV 10.4m

Arriva's HW4, one of five based at Wood Green heads past Old Street. *Photo: Peter Horrex*

Built: **Wrightbus**   Introduced: **2008 & 2009**   Number: **10**
Operators (routes): **Arriva (141), FIrst (328)**

N94UD - OmniDekka 10.6m

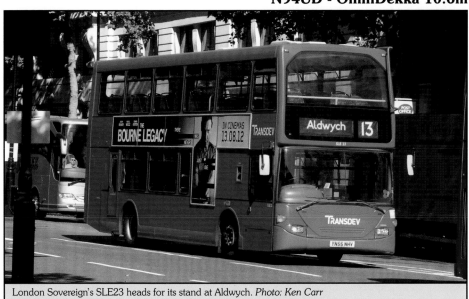

London Sovereign's SLE23 heads for its stand at Aldwych. *Photo: Ken Carr*

Built: **Scania/East Lancs**   Introduced: **2003-2006**   Number: **233**
Operators (routes): **Go-Ahead (*425*, 474), London Sovereign (13 114, *183*, 292), London United (27, 267, *281*), Metrobus (64, 119, 127, 161, 261, 320, 353, 405)**

N230UD - Olympus 10.8m

SEL759 heads around the one-way system at Marble Arch. *Photo: Peter Horrex*

Built: **Scania/East Lancs, Scania/Optare**   Introduced: **2007-2009**   Number: **63**
Operators (routes): **Metrobus (54, 75), Metroline (7, *79*, 297)**

N230UD - OmniCity 10.8m

The Polish-built OmniCitys have become a common sight since several companies ordered them in quantity. London United's SP113 picks up at Marble Arch. *Photo: Jack Marian*

Built: **Scania**   Introduced: **2008-2010**   Number: **420**
Operators (routes): **CT Plus (212), First (207), Go-Ahead (425, 474), London Sovereign (13, 114, 183, 292), London United (10, 49, 65, 71, 111, 120, 131, 148, 267, 281, 482, H32, H91), Metrobus (64, 119, 320), Stagecoach (48, 51, 53, 55, 56, 96, 106, 177, 205, 215, 248)**

LT7 approaches Victoria. Along with the other 'Borismasters' it is being used on extra route 38 workings whilst they are being evaluated. *Photo: Ken Carr*

Built: **Wrightbus**
Operators (routes): **Arriva (38)**

Introduced: **2012**

Number: **8**

Routemaster

Routemasters are used on two heritage routes on a daily basis. This is First's RM1913 a regular on route 9H from High Street Kensington to Trafalgar Square. *Photo: Ken Carr*

Built: **AEC**   Introduced: **1959-1967**   Number: **19**
Operators (routes): **First (9H), Stagecoach (15H)**

Trident - ALX400 9.9m

Two of the 9.9 metre Trident ALX400s head along Stratford Broadway. *Photo: Ken Carr*

Built: **Dennis/Alexander, TransBus, Alexander Dennis**   Introduced: **1999-2005**   Number: **403**
Operators (routes): **Abellio** (172, *344*, 350, 407, C3), **London United** (57, *65*, *71*, *111*, 131, *267*, 281, 371),
Stagecoach (69, *97*, *115*, 122, *147*, *241*, 247, 257, 262, 294, 330, *472*, 473, *496*)

Trident - ALX400 10.5m

17937 turns into West Ham Lane at Stratford working route 69. *Photo: Ken Carr*

Built: **Dennis/Alexander, TransBus, Alexander Dennis**   Introduced: **1999-2003/05/06**   Number: **401**
Operators (routes): **First (*295*,), London United (94, 220), Metroline (*16*, 32), Stagecoach (5, 8, 15, 47, *48*, 55, *56*, 69, 86, 97, *99*, *101*, 103, 104, 115, 122, 158, *205*, 208, 230, *238*, 241, *247*, 257, 269, 277, *330*, 472)**

Trident - Lolyne 10.0m

This combination is only operated by CT Plus, all ten can be found on the 388. *Photo: Ken Carr*

Built: **TransBus/East Lancs**   Introduced: **2003**   Number: **10**
Operators (routes): **CT Plus** (388)

Trident (Enviro400) - Olympus 10.3m

These Olympus bodied buses use the Enviro400 chassis. CT Plus has one, the rest operate for Go-Ahead
Photo: Peter Horrex

Built: **Alexander Dennis/East Lancs, Alexander Dennis/Optare**   Introduced: **2008 & 2009**   Number: **55**
Operators (routes): **CT Plus (388), Go-Ahead (93, 151, 154, *213*)**

Trident - President 9.9m

Another type that is starting to decline in numbers. First's TN33184 picks-up in Harrow Road. *Photo: Jack Marion*

Built: **Dennis/Plaxton, TransBus**   Introduced: **1999-2003**   Number: **189**
Operators (routes): **CT Plus (*388*), First (58, *92*, U3, U4), Go-Ahead (*67*), Metroline (*4*, 17, *32*, *43*, *139*, 217, 237, 263, 271, 603, E8, W8)**

TPL278 is based at Potters Bar and is a regular on the 82. Here it passes through Golders Green. *Photo: Ken Carr*

Built: **Dennis/Plaxton, TransBus**   Introduced: **2000-2002**   Number: **110**
Operators (routes): **First (58, *92*), Go-Ahead (*259, 476*) Metroline (*4*, 16, 43, 82, *134, 140, 182*)**

The Garages

Bus garages in the London area come in all shapes, sizes and ages. Some are located on High Streets, others in anonymous industrial parks.

Some are traditional bus garages (i.e. built for buses) such as Sutton, others are former tram and trolleybus depots, like Holloway. This opened as a tram shed, but was then converted to a trolleybus depot before finally becoming a bus garage. Newer garages have been created inside industrial units, such as Beddington Cross.

Speaking of which, Arriva has recently mothballed its facility (CN) at Beddington. Go-Ahead has acquired Northumberland Park garage from First, while First itself has opened a new site at Atlas Road as overflow parking while the main Westbourne Park garage is disrupted by Crossrail work.

The biggest garage in London (the biggest in Britain, for that matter) is the new West Ham, opened in 2008 with capacity for more than 300 buses.

Each garage has a one- or two-letter code, used by London Buses for administrative purposes. Operators also give garages their own codes, which, in most cases but not always, are the same as the ones assigned by London Buses. Within the book, we've used operators' codes exclusively, as these are the ones you're likely to see on the buses themselves. For the sake of completeness, where the code is different, it's shown in the following listing in parentheses underneath the operator's code.

The continued use of different coding systems from different eras means there is no uniformity. Many were created to a system introduced in the early part of the 20th Century by the London General Omnibus Company, which allocated codes alphabetically - A, B, C, etc., then AA, AB, AC, etc. So, Sutton became

A and Camberwell was Q . . . which doesn't make a huge amount of sense. Later codes are a little more user-friendly, for example PM for **P**eckha**m**.

Since the start of the tendering period in 1985, some codes have reflected the name of the owning company. BE, for instance, refers to Blue Triangle at Rainham. Some of these later additions have been retained as the building's code when the original operator has ceased to be – a system which, perversely, can also be traced back to the very earliest codes. As an example, the Tilling company had three garages at Bromley, Croydon and Lewisham which became TB, TC and TL. So far, so good, but it doesn't explain why TL is referred to as Catford in the modern world. Equally baffling at first sight is Abellio's garage at Battersea – QB – which actually stands for Q-Drive Battersea after the operator when the location was first used.

Some codes have been used for more than one garage over the years, or for different buildings in the same area. A new garage at Peckham, for instance, remained PM. There are other instances of codes lying dormant for many years before resurrection in a completely different area. Readers of a certain age will remember code C as Athol Street, Poplar . . . not Metrobus, Croydon.

Currently, three garages are shared by two companies in the same building and . . . yes, you've guessed . . . using different codes:

Edgware is both EW (the original code used by Metroline) and BT (used by London Sovereign).

Fulwell - FW (correct code used by London United) and TF (Abellio).

Ash Grove - AE (Arriva) and HK (CT Plus).

In conclusion, then, it's mad. Let us move on.

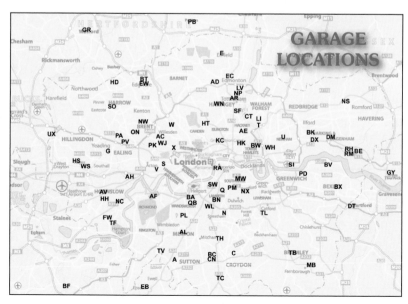

Code	Garage	Address/*Routes Operated*/Buses Allocated	PVR	Operator
A	Sutton	Bushey Road, Sutton, SM1 1QJ *80 93 151 154 164 213 413 N155* B7TL/Pres 10.0m, Dart/Est 10.4m, Dart/Point 10.1m, Env200 (E) 10.2m, Env400, Tri/Olym 10.3m.	82	Go-Ahead
AC	Willesden	287 High Road, Willesden, London, NW10 2JY *6 52 98 260 302 460 N52* B7TL/Pres 10.0m, B7TL/Pres 10.6m.	120	Metroline
AD	Palmers Green	Regents Avenue, London, N13 *34 102 125 329 629 634* DB250/Pres 10.2m, Env400.	55	Arriva
AE	Ash Grove	Mare Street, South Hackney, London, E8 *38 78 168 254 393* B7TL/Gem 10.1m, B7TL/Gem 10.6m, DB250/ALX400 10.2m, Dart/ALX200 10.2m, Dart/Point2 10.7m, Env200 9.3m, Env400, NBfL	79	Arriva
AF	Putney	10 Chelverton Road, London, SW15 1RN *14 22 74 85 424 430 N22 N74* B7TL/Gem 10.1m, B9TL/Env400 10.4m, Dart/Point 8.8m.	112	Go-Ahead
AH	Brentford	Commerce Road, Brentford, Middlesex, TW8 8LZ *190 209 237 E2 E8 609 635* B9TL/Gem2, Dart/Evo 10.2m, Env200 10.2m, OPTempH 10.6m, Tri/Pres 9.9m.	72	Metroline
AL	Merton	High Street, London, SW19 1DN *44 77 118 155 163 164 200 201 219 249 270 280 655 N155* B7TL/Gem 10.1m, B7TL/Pres 10.0m, B9TL/Gem2 (E), Dart/Est 10.4m, Dart/Point 8.8m, Dart/Point 10.1m, SB120/Cad 9.4m, Env200 10.2m, ENV400, Env400 (E).	162	Go-Ahead
AR	Tottenham	Philip Lane, High Cross, London, N15 *41 76 123 149 243 N41 N76* B5LH/Gem2 10.4m, B7TL/ALX400 10.1m, DB250/ALX400 10.2m, DB300/Gem2 10.4m.	128	Arriva

Tottenham garage was opened in 1913. Currently operated by Arriva the garage can hold around 125 buses.
Photo: Ken Carr

AS Atlas Road
Atlas Road, Harlesden, London, NW10
28 31 266 328 N28 N31
B7TL/Gem 10.1m, B7TL/Gem 10.6m, B9TL/Gem 2 (E), Gem2 HEV.
98 First

AV Hounslow
Kingsley Road, Hounslow
81 111 120 203 222 696 697 H32 H37 H98 N9
B7TL/ALX400 10.1m, B7TL/Pres 10m, Cit, CN94UD/Omni 10.7m,
Dart/Point2 10.1m, Env200 10.8m, ENV400 (E), N230UD/Omni 10.8m,
OPTemp 12.0m, Tri/ALX400 9.9m.
126 London United

BC Beddington
Unit 10, Beddington Cross, Beddington Farm Road, Croydon, CR0 4XH
152 157 322 407 434 455 931 P13 T33
B7TL/Gem 10.6m, Dart/Nimb 10.5m, Dart/Point 8.8m,
Dart/Point2 10.1m, Env200 8.9m, Env200 10.2m, Env200 10.8m,
Tri/ALX400 9.9m.
79 Abellio

Abellio's Beddington garage is located on an industrial estate to the west of Croydon. It was opened in 2000.
Photo: Jack Marian

BE Rainham
Unit 3C, Denver Trading Estate, Ferry Lane, Rainham, Essex, RM13 9BU
20 167 300 347 362 364 376 462 649 650 651 674 EL1 EL2 W19
B9TL/Gem2, B9TL/Gem2 (E), Dart/Evo 9.2m, Dart/Evo 10.4m,
Env200 10.2m, Env200 10.8m, Street WF.
90 Go-Ahead

BK Barking
205 Longbridge Road, Barking, Essex, IG11 8UE
5 62 101 145 169 366 387 396 687 N15
Env200 10.2m, Env400, Env400 (E), OPVer 10.4m, Tri/ALX400 10.5m.
114 Stagecoach

BN Brixton
39 Streatham Hill, London, SW2
50 59 109 137 159 319 N109
B7TL/ALX400 10.1m, DB250/ALX400 10.2m, DB250/ Gem,
DB300/Gem2, Env400.
139 Arriva

BT Edgware
Approach Road, Edgware, Middlesex, HA8 7AN
13 114 183 251 292 324 605 N13
B7TL/Pres 10.6m, B7TL/Vyk 11.0m, Env200 8.9m, Env200 10.2m,
N94UD/Omni 10.6m, N230UD/Omni 10.8m.
82 Lon. Sovereign

BV Belvedere
Burts Wharf, Crabtree Manorway North, Belvedere, DA17 6BT
180 244 669 N1
B7TL/Gem 10.6m, Env200 10.2m.
27 Go-Ahead

105

Code Garage	Address/*Routes Operated*/Buses Allocated	PVR	Operator
BW Bow	Fairfield Road, Bow, London, E3 2QP *8 15 205 277 N8* Env 400H (E), N230UD/Omni 10.8m, Tri/ALX400 10.5m.	**99**	**Stagecoach**
BX Bexleyheath	Erith Road, Bexleyheath, Kent, DA7 6BX *89 132 229 321 401 422 486 625 658 661 B11 B16 N21 N89* B7TL/Pres 10.0m, B9TL/Gem2, Dart/Point 10.1m, Env200 10.2m, Env400, Env400 (E), SB120/Cad 9.4m, SB120/Cad 9.4m, SB120/Cad 10.8m.	**114**	**Go-Ahead**
C Croydon	134 Beddington Lane, Beddington, CR9 4ND *54 64 75 119 127 130 202 293 359 405 612 N64 T32* 14.240/Env200 10.7m, 14.240/Evo 10.8m, Dart/Point 10.7m, Dart/Point2 10.7m, N94UD/Omni 10.6m, N230UD/Olym 10.8m, N230UB/Omni 12.0m, N230UD/Omni 10.8m.	**110**	**Metrobus**
CT Clapton	15 Bohemia Place, Mare Street, London, E8 *38 242 393 N38* B7TL/Gem 10.1m, DB300/Gem2, DB300/Gem2 (E), Env200 9.3m, Env400.	**99**	**Arriva**
DM Dagenham **(RN)**	73 Chequers Lane, Dagenham, Essex, RM9 6QJ *58 165 179 193 252 365 368 498 608 646 648 652 656 667 679 686 953* B7TL/Gem 10.1m, Dart/Cap 8.9m, Dart/Cap 9.3m, Dart/Cap 10.2m, Env200 10.2m, Env400, Tri/Pres 9.9m, Tri/Pres 10.5m.	**84**	**First**
DT Dartford	Central Road, Dartford, Kent, DA1 *126 160 233 286 428 492 B12 B13 B15* Dart/Point2 10.7m, DB250/Gem, Env200 8.9m, Env200 10.2m, Env200 10.8m, Enviro400 (E), SB120/Cad 9.4m.	**71**	**Arriva Southern** **Counties**
DX Barking	Ripple Road, Barking *128 135 150 173 325 647 678* B7TL/ALX400 10.1m, Env200 10.2m, Env400.	**63**	**Arriva**

One of Quality Line's Optare Solos, OP23 receives attention in the maintenance shed at the company's Epsom garage. *Photo: Jack Marian*

Code	Garage	Address/*Routes Operated*/Buses Allocated	PVR	Operator
E	Enfield	Southbury Road, Ponders End, EN1 *121 279 307 313 317 327 349 377 491 N279* B7TL/Gem 10.1m, Dart/Point 8.8m, DB250/ALX400 10.2m, DB250/ALX400 10.6m, DB250/Pres 10.2m, Env200 10.2m, Env200 (E) 10.8m, Env400 (E)	107	Arriva
EB	Epsom	Blenheim Road, Epsom, Surrey, KT19 9AF *404 406 411 418 463 465 467 470 641 K5 S1 S3 S4 X26* Cit, Dart/ALX200 8.9m, Dart/Lancs 9.0m, E200/Est 9.5m, E200/Lancs 9.0m, Env200 8.9m, Env400, OPSolo 8.5m, OPSolo 8.8m, OPVer 11.1m.	72	Quality Line
EW	Edgware	Approach Road, Edgware, Middlesex, HA8 7AN *107 113 186 204 240 606 N5 N98 N113* B7TL/Pres 10.6m, Env400.	70	Metroline
FW	Fulwell	Wellington Road, Fulwell, Middlesex, TW2 5NX *65 71 110 131 216 267 281 371 671 681 691* Dart/Point2 10.1m, Env200 10.2m, Env200H 10.2m, N94UD/Omni 10.6m, N230UD/Omni 10.8m, Tri/ALX400 9.9m.	125	London United
G	Greenford	Council Depot, Greenford Road, Greenford *92 95 282 E1 E3 E5 E7 E9 E10* B7TL/Gem 10.6m, Env200 8.9m, Env200 10.2m, Env400, Tri/Pres 9.9m, Tri/Pres 10.5m.	117	First
GR	Watford	934 St. Albans Road, Watford, Hertfordshire, WD2 6NN *142 258 268 288 303 305 340 642 H1 H2 H3 H18 H19* B6BLE/Cru, Dart/Point 10.2m, DB250/ALX400 10.2m, DB250/Gem 10.3m, DB300/Gem2, OPSolo 7.8m, SB120/Cad 10.2m.	71	Arriva The Shires
GY	Grays	Unit 7, Europa Park, London Road, Grays, Essex, RM20 4DB *66 256 346 370 375 499* Dar/Point 9.3m, DB250/ALX400 10.2m, Env200 10.2m, Env200 10.8m, SB120/Cad 10.2m.	38	Arriva Southern Counties
HD	Harrow Weald	467 High Road, Harrow Weald, Middlesex, HA3 6EJ *140 182 H12 N16* B7TL/Pres 10.0m, B7TL/Pres 10.6m, Tri/Pres 10.5m.	58	Metroline
HH (WK)	Hounslow Heath	Tamian Way, Hounslow, Middlesex, TW4 6BL *116 285 423 482 698 H22 H91* Dart/Point2 10.1m, Env200 10.2m, Env200 10.8m, N230UD/Omni 10.8m, Env400H.	70	London United
HK	Ash Grove	Mare Street, South Hackney, London, E8 *153 212 309 385 388 394 675 W5 W12 W13* Dart/Nim 8.9m, Dart/Nim 10.5m, Dart/Point 8.8m, E200/Est 9.4m, Env200 8.9m, N230UD/Omni 10.8m, OPSolo 8.8m, OPSolo 9.6m, OP Solo SE 7.8m, Tri/Loyl 10.0m, Tri/Olym 10.3m, Tri/Pres 9.9m.	69	CT Plus
HS (HZ)	Hayes	Swallowfield Way, Hayes *195 207 427 N207* B9TL/Gem2, Env200 10.2m, N230UD/Omni 10.8m.	71	First
HT	Holloway	37A Pemberton Gardens, London, N19 5RR *4 17 43 91 134 271 390 603 N5 N20 N91 W7* B7TL/Pres 10m, B7TL/Pres 10.6m, B9TL/Gem2 (E), Env400, Tri/Pres 9.9m, Tri/Pres 10.5m.	168	Metroline
KC	King's Cross	Freight Lane, London N1 *46 214 274* Dart/Point2 10.1m, Env200 10.2m.	52	Metroline
LI (HO)	Lea Interchange	151 Ruckholt Road, Leyton, London, E10 5PB *25 26 30 58 236 308 339 N26 RV1 W14 W15* B9TL/Gem2, Dart/Cap 9.3m, Dart/Cap 10.2m, Dart/Nim 10.5m, Env200 9.3m, Env200 10.2m, Env200 (E) 9.6m, Env400, Puls2Hydro.	182	First
LV	Leeside Road	Leeside Road, Tottenham, N17 *34 192 318 341 379 397 444 657 W3 W6 W11* Dart/ALX200 9.4m, Dart/Point 8.8m, Dart/Point 9.3m, DB250/ALX400 10.2m, Env200 (E) 8.9m, Env200 (E) 9.6m, Env400, Env400 (E), SB120/Cadet 10.2m	110	Arriva

Code	Garage	Address/*Routes Operated*/Buses Allocated	PVR	Operator

MB Orpington — Oak Farm, Farnborough Hill, Green Street Green, Orpington, Kent, BR6 6DA
138 146 161 162 181 261 284 320 336 352 353 358 367 464 654
B14 R1 R2 R3 R4 R5 R6 R7 R8 R9 R10 R11   **158 Metrobus**
12.240/Lancs 10.3m, Dart/Cap 8.9m, Dart/Cap 10.2m, Dart/Est 9.0m,
Dart/Point 8.8m, Env200 8.9m, Env200 10.2m, Env200 (E) 8.9m,
N94UB/Omni 12.0m, N94UB/Est 10.6m, N94UD/Omni 10.6m,
N230UD/Omni 10.8m, OPSolo SE 7.1m

MW Mandela Way East — Mandela Way, SE1 5SS
1 453 521 624 N1   **58 Go-Ahead**
B7TL/Gem 10.6m, Cit, Env400.

N Norwood — Knights Hill, London, SE27
2 133 176 415 417 432 690 N137   **118 Arriva**
B7TL/ALX400 10.1m, B7TL/ALX400 10.6m, DB250/ALX400 10.2m,
Env400.

Opened in 1909, Norwood garage was rebuilt between 1981 and 1984. Today it has a capacity of just under 150 buses. Photo: *David McKay*

NC Twickenham — Twickenham Trading Estate, Rugby Road, Twickenham, Middlesex, TW1 1DU
33 419   **25 London United**
Dart/Point2 10.1m, Env200 10.2m.

NP Northumberland Park — Marsh Lane, Tottenham, London, N17
67 191 231 259 299 357 389 399 476 616 692 699 W4 W10 W16   **117 Go-Ahead**
B7TL/Pres 10.6m, B9TL/Gem2, Dart/Cap 8.9m, Env200 8.9m,
Env200 9.3m, Env200 (E) 9.6m, Env400, Tri/Pres 9.9m, Tri/Pres 10.5m.

NS Romford — North Street, Romford, Essex, RM1 1DS
86 103 175 247 294 296 496 N86   **90 Stagecoach**
Env200 10.2m, Env400, Tri/ALX400 9.9m, Tri/ALX400 10.5m.

NX New Cross — 208 New Cross Road, London, SE14
21 36 108 129 171 225 321 436 621 N21 N171   **151 Go-Ahead**
B7TL/Pres 10.0m, B9TL/Gem2, Dart/Evo 10.8m, Dart/Point 10.1m,
Env400H (E), Env400, Env400H, SB120/Cad 10.8m.

ON Alperton   Ealing Road, Alperton, Middlesex, HA0
83 223 224 245 487   **75 First**
B7TL/Gem 10.1m, B9TL/Gem2, Env200 (E) 9.6m, Env200 10.2m.

PA Perivale   Unit 12, Perivale IndusTrial Park, Horsenden Lane Sth, Greenford, UB6 7RL
(West)   *7 79 90 105 297 395 611 E6 N7*   **101 Metroline**
B9TL/Gem2, B9TL/Gem2 (E), Env200 10.2m, Env200 (E) 10.2m,
MAN12.240/Evo 10.4m N230UD/Olym 10.8m.

PB Potters Bar   High Street, Potters Bar, Herts, EN6 5BE
82 217 234 263 383 384 626 N20 N91 W8 W9   **99 Metroline**
Dart/Point 9.3m, Env200 8.9m, Env200 (E) 9.6m, Env400,
Tri/Pres 9.9m, Tri/Pres 10.5m.

At Potters Bar, TE936's work for the day is complete, whilst TE950 will be working the night shift. *Photo: Peter Horrex*

PD Plumstead   Pettman Crescent, Plumstead, London, SE28 0BJ
51 53 96 99 122 177 291 386 469 472 601 602 672   **161 Stagecoach**
Dart/Point 9.3m, Env200 9.3m, Env200 10.2m, Env400,
N230UD/Omni 10.8m, Tri/ALX400 9.9m, Tri/ALX400 10.5m.

PK Park Royal   Atlas Road, Harlesden, London, NW10 6DN
272 283 440 C1 E11   **53 London United**
Env200 8.9m, Env200 10.2m, OPVer 10.4m.

PL Waterside   Waterside Way, London, SW17 0HB
Way   *39 485 493 G1*   **44 Go-Ahead**
Dart/Point 8.8m, Dart/Point 10.1m, Env200 (E) 10.2m.

PM Peckham   Blackpool Road, Peckham, London, SE15 3SE
37 63 363 N63 P12 X68   **71 Go-Ahead**
B7TL/Pres 10.0m, B9TL/Gem2, Env200 (E) 10.2m, Env400.

109

Plumstead's MOT shed plays host to an ALX400 and two Versas which would transfer to Barking upon receipt of their certificates. *Photo: Ken Carr*

Code	Garage	Address/*Routes Operated*/Buses Allocated	PVR	Operator
Q	Camberwell	1 Warner Road, Camberwell, London, SE5 9LU *12 42 45 68 185 345 355 360 468 N68 P5 X68* B5LH/Gem2, B7TL/Gem 10.1m, B7TL/Gem 10.6m, B7TL/Pres 10.0m, Dart/Point2 10.1m, Electy 10.3m, Electy 10.4m, Env200 9.3m, N94UB/Lanc 10.6m, OPVers Hybrid.	204	Go-Ahead
QB	Battersea	Silverthorne Road, Battersea, London, SW8 3HE *3 156 211 344 414 452 C2 C3 C10 N3* Env200 10.2m, Env400, Env400 (E), Env400H (E), Tri/ALX400 9.9m.	163	Abellio
RA	Waterloo	Cornwall Road, London, SE1 8TE *507 521* Cit.	40	Go-Ahead
RM	Rainham	Unit 2, Albright Industrial Estate, Ferry Lane, Rainham, Essex, RM13 9BU *174 248 287 372* Env200 10.8m, Env400, N230UD/Omni 10.8m.	47	Stagecoach
S	Shepherd's Bush	Wells Road, London, W12 *49 72 94 148 220* B7TL/ALX400 10.1m, B7TL/Vyk 10.4m, Env200 10.2m, Env400H, N230UD/Omni 10.8m, Tri/ALX400 10.5m.	115	London United
SF	Stamford Hill	Rookwood Road, London N16 *73 253 N73 N253* B5LH/Gem2, B7TL/Gem 10.1m, B7TL/Gem 10.6m, DB250/ALX400 10.2m, DB300/Gem2 (E).	78	Arriva
SI	Silvertown	Factory Road, Silvertown, London, E16 *276 425 474 549 673 D6 D7 D8 N551* B9TL/Gem2, B9TL/MCV, Dart/Evo 10.4m, Env200 10.8m, Env200 (E) 10.2m, N94UD/Omni 10.6m, N230UD/Omni 10.8m.	78	Go-Ahead
SM	South Mimms	331 Pinner Road, Harrow *298 628 653 683 688* B7TL/Gem 10.6m, B7TL/Pres 10.5m, B7TL/Vyk 10.4m, Env200 (E) 10.2m, Tri/Lol 10m, Tri/Pres 10.5m	16	Sullivans
SO	Harrow	331 Pinner Road, Harrow *398 H9 H10 H11 H13 H14 H17* Dart/Point 10.1m, Dart/Point2 10.1m, Env200 10.2m.	43	Lon. Sovereign
SW	Stockwell	Binfield Road, London, SW4 6ST *11 19 24 87 88 170 196 315 333 337 639 670 N11 N19 N44 N87* B5LH/Gem2, B7TL/Gem 10.1m, B7TL/Pres 10.0m, B9TL/Gem2 (E), Dart/Point 8.8m, Dart/Point 10.7m, Env200 10.8m, Env400, Env400H, DB300/Gem2.	187	Go-Ahead

Stockwell garage has 6,814 square metres of unobstructed parking, and can hold around 200 buses. Opened in 1952 the garage was designed by Adie, Button and Partners. *Photo: David McKay*

111

Code	Garage	Address/*Routes Operated*/Buses Allocated	PVR	Operator
T	Leyton	High Road, Leyton, London, E10 6AD *48 55 56 97 215 230 275 N55* Env400 (E), N230UD/Omni 10.8m, Tri/ALX400 10.5m.	105	Stagecoach
TB	Bromley	111 Hastings Road, Bromley, Kent, BR2 8NH *61 208 227 246 269 314 354 636 637 638 664* Cit, Env200 8.9m, Env200 10.8m, Env200 (E) 10.2m, Env 400, Env400 10.8m, Tri/ALX400 10.5m.	82	Stagecoach
TC	Croydon	Brighton Road, Croydon, CR2 6EL *60 166 194 197 264 312 403 412 466 627 685 N133 T31* Dart/Point 10.1m, DB250/ALX400 10.2m, DB250/Gem, Env200 10.2m, Env400.	117	Arriva
TF	Fulwell	The Old Tram Depot, Stanley Road, Twickenham, Middlesex, TW2 5NP *117 235 290 481 490 969 H20 H25 H26 R68 R70* Dart/Nimb 10.5m, Dart/Nimb 11m, Dart/Point 8.8m, Env200 8.9m, Env200 10.2m, Env200 (E) 10.2m, Env200 (E) 10.8m, Electy 10.3m.	86	Abellio
TH	Thornton Heath	719 London Road, Thornton Heath *198 250 255 289 410 450* Dart/Point 9.3m, Dart/Point2 10.7m, DB250/ALX400 10.2m, DB250/ALX400 10.6m, Env200 (E) 10.8m, Env400, SB120/Cad 10.2m.	85	Arriva
TL	Catford	180 Bromley Road, Catford, London, SE6 2XA *47 124 136 178 199 273 356 380 660 N136 P4* Dart/ALX200 8.9m, Dart/Point 8.8m, Dart/Point 10.1m, Dart/Point2 10.1m, Env200 8.9m, Env200 (E) 8.9m, Env400, Env400 (E), OPTempH, Tri/ALX400 10.5m.	97	Stagecoach

A trio of ALX400s receive attention in Stagecoach's Catford garage. *Photo: Jack Marian*

Code	Garage	Address/*Routes Operated*/Buses Allocated	PVR	Operator
TV	Tolworth	Kingston Road, Tolworth *57 265 613 665 965 K1 K2 K3 K4* Dart/Point2 8.8m, Dart/Point2 10.1m, Env200 8.9m, Tri/ALX400 9.9m.	74	London United
UX	Uxbridge	Bakers Road, Uxbridge *331 607 A10 U1 U2 U3 U4 U5 U10* B7TL/Gem 10.1m, Dart/Nim 10.5m, Env200 10.2m, Env400, Tri/Pres 9.9m.	86	First
V	Stamford Brook	72-74 Chiswick High Road, London, W4 *9 10 27 391* B7TL/Vyk 11.0m, N94UD/Omni 10.6m, N230UD/Omni 10.8m, OPVer 10.4m.	92	London United

Code	Garage	Address/*Routes Operated*/Buses Allocated	PVR	Operator
W	Cricklewood	329 Edgware Road, Dollis Hill, London, NW2 6JP *16 32 139 143 189 210 232 316 326 332 632 643 C11 N16* Dart/Point2 10.1m, Env200 10.2m, Env400, Env400 (E), Env400H, Env400H (E), Tri/ALX400 10.5m, Tri/Pres 9.9m, Tri/Pres 10.5m.	187	Metroline
WH	West Ham	Stephenson Street, Canning Town, London, E16 4SA *15H 69 97 104 106 115 147 158 238 241 257 262 323 330 473* *488 D3 N550* Env200 10.2m, Env400 10.8m, Env400H (E), N230UD/Omni 10.8m, RM, Tri/ALX400 9.9m, Tri/ALX400 10.5m.	209	Stagecoach
WJ	Willesden Junction	Station Road, Harlesden, NW10 *18 187 206 226 228 N18* B9TL/Gem2, Env200 10.2m, Env200 (E) 10.8m, Street DF.	99	First
WL	Walworth	301 Camberwell New Road, London, SE5 0TF *35 40 100 172 188 343 381 484 N35 N343 N381* B7TL/Gem 10.6m, Dart/Point2 9.4m, Env 200 9.3m, Env400, Env400H (E), Tri/ALX400 9.9m.	142	Abellio
WN	Wood Green	Jolly Butchers Hill, High Road, London, N22 *29 141 144 184 221 382 617 N29* B7TL/Gem 10.1m, Dart/Point 8.8m, DB250/ALX400 10.2m, DB250/ALX400 10.6m, DB300/Gem2 (E), Env200 10.2m, Env400 (E), Gem2HEV.	132	Arriva

Wood Green was originally built as a horse-tram garage and then in the early 1900s it converted to the electric version. In the 1930s it became a trolleybus depot before becoming a bus garage in 1962. *Photo: Ken Carr*

Code	Garage	Address/*Routes Operated*/Buses Allocated	PVR	Operator
WS	Hayes	West London Coach Centre, North Hyde Gardens, Hayes, UB3 4QT *112 350 H28 U7 U9* Dart/Nimb 10.5m, Dart/Point 8.8m, Dart/Point2 8.8m, Dart/Spry, Tri/ALX400 9.9m.	30	Abellio
X	Westbourne Park	Great Western Road, London, W9 *9H 23 70 295* B9TL/Gem2, DB300/Gem2, Env 200 (E) 10.2m, Env400 (E), Env400H (E), RMTri/ALX400 10.5m,	70	First

The Routes

It goes without saying that London has a wonderful variety of bus routes . . . and the capital boasts the best night-time service of any city in the world! As well as the night changeovers to N numbers (e.g. 35 to N35), other routes run 24 hours anyway and retain their usual identity (e.g. 24). The N routes are as a rule extended versions of the day route. Each route has its own Peak Vehicle Requirement based on service frequency, length and passenger numbers. Route 38, for instance, runs from Clapton to Victoria at 3 minute intervals in the rush hour and has the highest PVR of 70 (all Wrightbus Gemini integrals). Additional services on route 38 are being operated by NBfL.The longest routes are X26 from Heathrow to Croydon and N89 from Erith to Charing Cross - both 21 miles. As a general rule, routes running through Central London have higher PVRs.

The following pages take each route in turn and show details of requirements, frequency (Mon-Sat & Sun), operator, buses used and the garages they run from. Bus types shown in italics are not rostered for the route but appear quite frequently.

With roughly a fifth of London routes up for tender each year, there are bound to be numerous changes. This section is correct to 16th September 2012, but as companies helpfully announce changeovers in advance, we've also included details of known alterations in the coming months. New operators are shown where applicable. Some routes receiving new buses will retain their current operator.

There will also be temporary changes caused by roadworks diversions which, in some cases, can also mean a change of frequency and an adjustment to the PVR.

Route	Start Date	Change
4	29/09/2012	18 new d/d [some hybrid]
271	29/09/2012	existing d/d
103	13/10/2012	new & existing d/d
128	13/10/2012	existing d/d
175	13/10/2012	new & existing d/d
257	13/10/2012	Go-Ahead - existing d/d WVLs
22	20/10/2012	new Gemini 2 & B5 hybrid
220	20/10/2012	new Enviro 400
370	03/11/2012	existing d/d (route 160 DLAs)
24	10/11/2012	Metroline - new Gemini 2 & B5 hybrid
27	10/11/2012	new Enviro 400 hybrid
267	10/11/2012	existing d/d
419	10/11/2012	existing s/d
470	17/11/2012	new s/d
52	08/12/2012	new d/d (incl 12 hybrids)
29	12/01/2013	new d/d
141	12/01/2013	new d/d
329	12/01/2013	new d/d
41	02/02/2013	new & existing d/d

121	02/02/2013	new d/d
153	02/02/2013	new s/d
142	09/02/2013	existing d/d
H28	23/02/2013	new s/d
36	09/02/2013	new & existing d/d
233	23/02/2013	Metrobus - new s/d
138	16/03/2013	new s/d
161	16/03/2013	existing d/d
225	16/03/2013	existing s/d
284	16/03/2013	new s/d
126	23/03/2013	Metrobus - new s/d
424	06/04/2013	existing s/d PVR5
127	13/04/2013	existing d/d
67	27/04/2013	Arriva - new d/d
106	27/04/2013	Arriva -new d/d
485	04/05/2013	existing s/d
37	01/06/2013	existing d/d
44	01/06/2013	new & existing d/d
77	01/06/2013	new & existing d/d
87	01/06/2013	new & existing d/d
219	01/06/2013	new s/d
270	01/06/2013	new & existing d/d
386	01/06/2013	new & existing s/d
491	01/06/2013	new s/d
327	08/06/2013	exisiting d/d
231	08/06/2013	new & existing d/d
230	22/06/2013	new d/d

To be Awarded . . .

Route	Start Date	
268	June 2013	
216	June 2013	
K1	June 2013	
K2	June 2013	
K3	June 2013	
K4	June 2013	
425	July 2013	
143	July 2013	
288	Aug. 2013	
303	Aug. 2013	
305	Aug. 2013	
H18	Aug. 2013	
H19	Aug. 2013	
60	Aug. 2013	
166	Aug. 2013	
412	Aug. 2013	
466	Aug. 2013	
293	Aug. 2013	
404	Sept. 2013	
434	Sept. 2013	

No.	Route	PVR	Freq		Operator	Garage	Type Used
1	Canada Water - Tottenham Court Road Station	16	8	12	Go-Ahead	MW	B7TL/Gem
2	West Norwood - Marylebone Station	24	8	10	Arriva	N	B7TL/ALX400 Env400
3	Crystal Palace - Oxford Circus	22	8	12	Abellio	QB	Env400H
4	Archway - Waterloo	18	10	15	Metroline	HT	*B7TL/Pres* Env400 *Tri/Pres*
5	Romford - Canning Town	30	7	8	Stagecoach	BK	*Env400* Tri/ALX400
6	Willesden Garage - Aldwych	26	6	10	Metroline	AC	B7TL/Pres

VP527 approaches Trafalgar Square, having just travelled along The Strand. *Photo: Ken Carr*

No.	Route	PVR	Freq		Operator	Garage	Type Used
7	East Acton - Russell Square	23	8	12	Metroline	PA	N230/Olym
8	Bow - Oxford Circus	29	7	10	Stagecoach	BW	Tri/ALX400
9	Hammersmith - Aldwych	22	6	10	London United	V	B7TL/Vyk
	(Heritage service Kensington H.S. & Trafalgar Sq.)	5	20	20	First	X	RM
10	Hammersmith - King's Cross	25	8	12	London United	V	N230/Omni
11	Fulham - Liverpool Street	24	8	10	Go-Ahead	SW	B7TL/Gem
12	Dulwich Library - Oxford Circus	41	5	5	Go-Ahead	Q	B5LH/Gem2 B9TL/Gem2
13	Golders Green - Aldwych	20	8	12	Lon. Sovereign	BT	N94/Omni N230/Omni B7TL/Pres *B7TL/Vyk*
14	Putney Heath - University College Hospital	34	6	10	Go-Ahead	AF	B7TL/Gem
15	Blackwall Station - Piccadilly Circus	23	8	8	Stagecoach	BW	Env400H Tri/ALX400
	(Heritage service between Tower Hill & Trafalgar Sq.)	5	15	15	Stagecoach	WH	RM
16	Cricklewood - Victoria	22	6	10	Metroline	W	Env400 Env400H *Tri/ALX400* Tri/Pres

No.	Route	PVR	Freq		Operator	Garage	Type Used
17	Archway - London Bridge	16	8	15	Metroline	HT	B7TL/Pres Tri/Pres
18	Sudbury - Euston	48	4	7	First	WJ	B9TL/Gem2
19	Battersea Bridge - Finsbury Park	28	8	10	Go-Ahead	SW	B9TL/Gem2
20	Debden - Walthamstow	10	15	30	Go-Ahead	BE	B9TL/Gem2
21	Lewisham - Newington Green	25	7	12	Go-Ahead	NX	B7TL/Pres B9TL/Gem2
22	Putney Common - Piccadilly Circus	22	8	12	Go-Ahead	AF	B7TL/Gem2
23	Westbourne Park - Liverpool Street	31	7	10	First	X	Env400 Env400H
24	Hampstead Heath - Pimlico	27	6	8	Go-Ahead	SW	Env400 Env400H

In November 2012 route 24 will move back to Metroline and will be operated by Gemini 2s. Go-Ahead currently operates this route with Enviro400s. With three months left on this route E66 passes the Victoria Palace theatre. *Photo: Peter Horrex*

No.	Route	PVR	Freq		Operator	Garage	Type Used
25	Ilford - Oxford Circus	59	4	5	First	LI	B9TL/Gem2
26	Hackney Wick - Waterloo	17	10	12	First	LI	Env400
27	Turnham Green - Camden Town	27	8	12	London United	V	B7TL/Vyk N94/Omni
28	Wandsworth - Kensal Rise	22	8	10	First	AS	B7TL/Gem
29	Wood Green Station - Trafalgar Square	42	5	5	Arriva	WN	B7TL/Gem DB300/Gem2 Env400
30	Hackney Wick - Marble Arch	23	10	12	First	LI	Env400
31	White City - Camden Town	24	6	6	First	AS	B7TL/Gem

No.	Route	PVR	Freq		Operator	Garage	Type Used
32	Edgware - Kilburn	17	8	12	Metroline	W	Env400
							Tri/ALX400
							Tri/Pres
33	Fulwell - Hammersmith	18	8	15	London United	NC	Env200
34	Barnet - Walthamstow	20	8	12	Arriva	LV	DB250/ALX400
						AD	DB250/Pres
							Env400
35	Clapham Junction - Shoreditch	19	10	15	Abellio	WL	Env400
36	New Cross Gate - Queens Park	33	6	12	Go-Ahead	NX	B7TL/Pres
							Env400
37	Putney Heath - Peckham	19	10	12	Go-Ahead	PM	*B9TL/Gem2*
							Env400
38	Clapton - Victoria	70	3	5	Arriva	CT	DB300/Gem2
						AE	NBfL
39	Putney - Clapham Junction	15	8	12	Go-Ahead	PL	Dar/Point
40	Dulwich Library - Aldgate	16	8	15	Abellio	WL	Env400
41	Tottenham Hale - Archway	21	5	10	Arriva	AR	*B7TL/ALX400*
							DB250/ALX400
42	Denmark Hill - Bishopsgate	11	10	15	Go-Ahead	Q	Omni/Myll
43	Friern Barnet - London Bridge	34	8	10	Metroline	HT	B9TL/Gem2
							B7TL/Pres
							Tri/Pres

VW1243 was delivered to Holloway earlier in 2012 and is regularly used on Route 43 between Barnet and London Bridge. *Photo: Peter Horrex*

No.	Route	PVR	Freq		Operator	Garage	Type Used
44	Tooting Station - Victoria	16	10	15	Go-Ahead	AL	B7TL/Gem
							B7TL/Pres
							Env400
45	Clapham Park - King's Cross	22	8	15	Go-Ahead	Q	*B7TL/Gem*
							B7TL/Pres
46	Lancaster Gate - Farringdon Street	17	10	15	Metroline	KC	Env200

No.	Route	PVR	Freq	Operator	Garage	Type Used
47	Bellingham Catford Bus Garage - Shoreditch	18	10	15	Stagecoach	TL	Tri/ALX400
48	Walthamstow - London Bridge	21	8	12	Stagecoach	T	N230/Omni
							Tri/ALX400
49	Clapham Junction - White City	19	8	10	London United	S	*B7TL/ALX400*
							B7TL/Vyk
							N230/Omni
50	Croydon - Stockwell	15	12	20	Arriva	BN	*DB250/ALX400*
							DB250/Gem
							Env400
51	Orpington - Woolwich	17	10	15	Stagecoach	PD	N230/Omni
52	Willesden - Victoria	25	6	8	Metroline	AC	B7TL/Pres
53	Plumstead Station - Whitehall	27	8	10	Stagecoach	PD	Env400
							N230/Omni
54	Elmers End Station - Woolwich	14	12	15	Metrobus	C	N230/Olym
55	Leyton Green - Oxford Circus	29	7	10	Stagecoach	T	N230/Omni
							Tri/ALX400
56	Whipps Cross - Smithfield	21	7	8	Stagecoach	T	N230/Omni
							Tri/ALX400
57	Kingston - Clapham Park	26	8	12	London United	TV	Tri/ALX400
58	East Ham - Walthamstow	16	10	15	First	LI	B9TL/Gem2
						DM	Tri/Pres
59	Streatham Hill - King's Cross	23	7	12	Arriva	BN	*DB250/ALX400*
							DB250/Gem
							DB300/Gem2

Buses that operate on routes through Central London are prime candidates for the advert treatment. Brixton's DW279 promotes Visa as it comes off Waterloo Bridge. *Photo: Ken Carr*

No.	Route	PVR	Freq	Operator	Garage	Type Used
60	Old Coulsdon - Streatham Common	16	12	20	Arriva	TC	DB250/ALX400
							DB250/Gem
61	Chislehurst Gordon Arms - Bromley	11	15	20	Stagecoach	TB	Env400
62	Marks Gate - Gascoigne Estate	15	10	20	Stagecoach	BK	Env200
							Env400
							Versa
63	Honor Oak - King's Cross	27	6	8	Go-Ahead	PM	B7TL/Pres
							B9TL/Gem2
							Env400

No.	Route	PVR	Freq		Operator	Garage	Type Used
64	New Addington - Thornton Heath Bus Garage	14	8	15	Metrobus	C	*N94/Omni* *N230/Omni*
65	Kingston - Ealing	22	8	10	London United	FW	*N230/Omni* *Tri/ALX400*
66	Romford - Leytonstone	11	12	30	Arriva Sth Cou.	GY	*Env200*
67	Wood Green Station - Aldgate	15	10	12	Go-Ahead	NP	*B7TL/Pres* *Tri/Pres*
68	West Norwood - Euston	21	8	12	Go-Ahead	Q	*B7TL/Gem* *B7TL/Pres*
69	Walthamstow - Canning Town	17	8	12	Stagecoach	WH	*Tri/ALX400*
70	Acton - South Kensington	15	10	15	First	X	*Env200*
71	Chessington World of Adventures - Kingston	12	8	12	London United	FW	*N230/Omni* *Tri/ALX400*
72	Roehampton - East Acton	17	8	12	London United	S	*Env200*
73	Seven Sisters - Victoria	51	5	6	Arriva	SF	*Gem2INT* *B5L/Gem2*
74	Putney - Baker Street	21	8	10	Go-Ahead	AF	*B7TL/Gem*
75	Croydon - Lewisham	13	14	15	Metrobus	C	*N230/Olym*
76	Tottenham - Waterloo	22	8	12	Arriva	AR	*B5L/Gem2* *DB250/ALX400* *DB300/Gem2*
77	Tooting Station - Waterloo	16	10	12	Go-Ahead	AL	*B7TL/Gem* *B7TL/Pres*
78	Nunhead - Shoreditch	16	9	12	Arriva	AE	*Env400*
79	Edgware - Alperton	11	13	15	Metroline	PA	*B9TL/Gem2* *N230/Olym*
80	Belmont Highdown Prison - Hackbridge	10	12	20	Go-Ahead	A	*E200/Est* *Dar/Point*
81	Slough - Hounslow	13	12	20	London United	AV	*Env400*
82	North Finchley - Victoria	24	8	12	Metroline	PB	*Tri/Pres*
83	Ealing Hospital - Golders Green	28	8	10	First	ON	*B7TL/Gem* *B9TL/Gem2*

Route 83 is 13 miles in length and runs from West to North London with Gemini 2s. *Photo: Ken Carr*

No.	Route	PVR	Freq		Operator	Garage	Type Used
85	Kingston - Putney	15	8	10	Go-Ahead	AF	B7TL/Gem
							B9TL/Env400
86	Romford - Stratford	30	6	10	Stagecoach	NS	Tri/ALX400
87	Wandsworth - Aldwych	21	6	12	Go-Ahead	SW	B7TL/Gem
							B7TL/Pres
88	Clapham Common - Camden Town	22	8	12	Go-Ahead	SW	B7TL/Pres
							Env400
89	Slade Green - Lewisham	15	10	20	Go-Ahead	BX	B7TL/Pres
							Env400
90	Feltham - Northolt	16	10	20	Metroline	PA	Env200
							Man240/Evo
91	Crouch End - Trafalgar Square	19	8	10	Metroline	HT	Env400

TE926 is one of Holloway's batch of Enviro400s delivered in 2009. It has about 3/4 mile to go to its destination as it navigates Aldwych. *Photo: Ken Carr*

No.	Route	PVR	Freq		Operator	Garage	Type Used
92	Brent Park - Ealing Hospital	18	8	10	First	G	B7TL/Gem
							Env400
							Tri/Pres
93	North Cheam - Putney	21	7	10	Go-Ahead	A	B7TL/Pres
							Env400
							Tri/Olym
94	Acton Green - Piccadilly Circus	30	5	8	London United	S	Env400H
							Tri/ALX400
95	Southall - Shepherd's Bush	14	12	20	First	G	Env200
96	Bluewater - Woolwich	21	8	12	Stagecoach	PD	N230/Omni
97	Chingford - Stratford City	20	8	12	Stagecoach	WH/T	Tri/ALX400
98	Willesden - Holborn	26	6	8	Metroline	AC	B7TL/Pres
99	Bexleyheath - Woolwich	12	12	15	Stagecoach	PD	Env400
							Tri/ALX400
100	Shadwell - Elephant & Castle	18	8	12	Abellio	WL	Env200
							Dar/Point

No.	Route	PVR	Freq		Operator	Garage	Type Used
101	Wanstead - Gallions Reach Shopping Park	11	12	15	Stagecoach	BK	Env400
							Tri/ALX400
102	Edmonton Green - Brent Cross	23	8	12	Arriva	AD	Env400
103	Chase Cross - Rainham	12	10	20	Stagecoach	NS	Tri/ALX400
104	Manor Park - Stratford	14	10	15	Stagecoach	WH	Env400
							Tri/ALX400
105	Greenford Station - Heathrow Airport Central	16	10	15	Metroline	PA	B9TL/Gem2
106	Finsbury Park - Whitechapel	18	8	10	Stagecoach	WH	N230/Omni
107	New Barnet Station - Edgware	9	15	20	Metroline	EW	B7TL/Pres
108	Lewisham - Stratford	14	10	15	Go-Ahead	NX	Dar/Evo
							Dar/Point
							SB120/Cadet
109	Croydon - Brixton	25	6	10	Arriva	BN	DB250/ALX400
							Env400
110	Twickenham - West Middlesex Hospital	5	20	30	London United	FW	Dar/Point
111	Heathrow Airport Central - Kingston	23	10	12	London United	AV	B7TL/ALX400
							N230/Omni
							Tri/ALX400
112	Ealing - Brent Cross	7	15	20	Abellio	WS	Dar/Nimb
113	Edgware - Marble Arch	18	10	20	Metroline	EW	B7TL/Pres
							Env400
114	Ruislip - Mill Hill	17	10	12	Lon. Sovereign	BT	B7TL/Pres
							B7TL/Vyk
							N94/Omni
							N230/Omni
115	East Ham - Aldgate	19	8	10	Stagecoach	WH	Tri/ALX400
116	Ashford Hospital - Hounslow	6	12	20	London United	HH	Dar/Point
117	Staines - Isleworth	8	20	30	Abellio	TF	Env200
118	Morden - Brixton	12	12	20	Go-Ahead	AL	B7TL/Gem
							B7TL/Pres
							Env400
119	Bromley - Purley Way	16	10	15	Metrobus	C	N94/Omni
							N230/Omni
120	Northolt - Hounslow	16	10	12	London United	AV	B7TL/ALX400
							B7TL/Pres
							CN94/Omni
							Env400
							N230/Omni
							Tri/ALX400
121	Enfield Lock - Turnpike Lane Station	20	10	15	Arriva	E	DB250/ALX400
122	Plumstead Bus Garage - Crystal Palace	16	12	15	Stagecoach	PD	Tri/ALX400
123	Ilford - Wood Green Station	19	10	15	Arriva	AR	B7TL/ALX400
							DB250/ALX400
							DB300/Gem2
124	Eltham - Catford	11	12	20	Stagecoach	TL	Env200
125	Winchmore Hill - Finchley	12	10	15	Arriva	AD	DB250/Pres
126	Eltham - Bromley	10	10	20	Arriva Sth Cou.	DT	Dar/Point
127	Purley - Tooting	10	15	30	Metrobus	C	N94/Omni
128	Claybury - Romford	12	12	20	Arriva	DX	B7TL/ALX400
129	North Greenwich - Greenwich	4	12	20	Go-Ahead	NX	Dar/Evo
130	New Addington - Norwood Junction	8	15	30	Metrobus	C	Dar/Point
131	Kingston - Tooting	20	8	12	London United	FW	N230/Omni
							Tri/ALX400
132	Bexleyheath - North Greenwich	12	12	20	Go-Ahead	BX	SB120/Cadet
							Dar/Point
133	Streatham - Liverpool Street Station	30	7	12	Arriva	N	Env400
134	North Finchley - Tottenham Court Road	30	7	8	Metroline	HT	B7TL/Pres
							B9TL/Gem2
							Tri/Pres

No.	Route	PVR	Freq		Operator	Garage	Type Used
135	Crossharbour - Old Street Station	13	10	15	Arriva	DX	Env400
136	Grove Park - Peckham	13	10	15	Stagecoach	TL	Env400
137	Streatham Hill - Marble Arch	30	6	8	Arriva	BN	DB250/Gem DB300/Gem2
138	Coney Hall - Bromley	3	20	30	Metrobus	MB	Dar/Myll
139	West Hampstead - Waterloo	21	8	12	Metroline	W	Env400 Env400H *Tri/Pres*

Metroline ordered ten Hybrid Enviro400s in 2010 for use on Cricklewood's route 139. *Photo: Ken Carr*

No.	Route	PVR	Freq		Operator	Garage	Type Used
140	Harrow Weald - Heathrow Airport Central	24	8	12	Metroline	HD	B7TL/Pres *Tri/Pres*
141	Wood Green Station - London Bridge	25	7	12	Arriva	WN	B7TL/Gem DB250/ALX400 Gem2 HEV
142	Watford - Brent Cross	15	12	15	Arriva Shires	GR	DB250/ALX400
143	Brent Cross - Archway	12	12	15	Metroline	W	Env200
144	Edmonton Green - Muswell Hill	16	8	10	Arriva	WN	*B7TL/Gem* Env400
145	Dagenham - Leytonstone	15	12	20	Stagecoach	BK	Env400 Tri/ALX400
146	Downe - Bromley	1	60	60	Metrobus	MB	Dar/Myll
147	Ilford - Canning Town Station	18	8	10	Stagecoach	WH	Tri/ALX400
148	Denmark Hill - White City	25	8	10	London United	S	B7TL/ALX400 N230/Omni
149	Edmonton Green - London Bridge	36	8	8	Arriva	AR	B5L/Gem2 DB300/Gem2
150	Chigwell Row - Becontree Heath	12	12	20	Arriva	DX	Env400
151	Worcester Park - Wallington	13	10	20	Go-Ahead	A	*B7TL/Pres* Tri/Olym
152	New Malden - Pollards Hill	12	12	20	Abellio	BC	Dar/Point Env200

No.	Route	PVR	Freq		Operator	Garage	Type Used
153	Finsbury Park - Liverpool Street	10	12	15	CT Plus	HK	Dar/Nimb
154	Morden - Croydon	12	12	20	Go-Ahead	A	*B7TL/Pres* Tri/Olym
155	Tooting - Elephant & Castle	17	8	12	Go-Ahead	AL	B7TL/Gem B7TL/Pres
156	Wimbledon - Vauxhall	16	8	12	Abellio	QB	Env400
157	Morden - Crystal Palace	16	12	20	Abellio	BC	B7TL/Gem
158	Chingford Mount - Stratford	13	10	12	Stagecoach	WH	Env400 Tri/ALX400
159	Streatham - Paddington Basin	38	6	12	Arriva	BN	B7TL/ALX400 DB300/Gem2
160	Sidcup - Catford	11	15	20	Arriva Sth Cou.	DT	Env400
161	Chislehurst - North Greenwich	14	10	12	Metrobus	MB	N94/Omni
162	Eltham Station - Beckenham Junction	8	20	30	Metrobus	MB	Env200
163	Morden - Wimbledon	12	8	12	Go-Ahead	AL	E200/Est

Route 163 should be operated by Esteem bodied Enviro200s. However, on this occasion Dart Pointer LDP193 works the service through Wimbledon. *Photo: Peter Horrex*

164	Sutton - Wimbledon	12	10	15	Go-Ahead	AL	*Dar/Point* E200/Est
165	Abbey Wood Lane - Romford Brewery	11	12	20	First	DM	Env200
166	Epsom General Hospital - Croydon	8	20	30	Arriva	TC	*Dar/Point* Env200
167	Debden - Ilford	9	20	30	Go-Ahead	BE	E200/Evo
168	Hampstead Heath - Old Kent Road	20	7	10	Arriva	AE	B7TL/Gem Env400
169	Clayhall - Barking	12	10	15	Stagecoach	BK	Env400
170	Roehampton - Victoria	19	8	12	Go-Ahead	SW	Dar/Point Env200
171	Bellingham Catford Bus Garage - Holborn	24	8	12	Go-Ahead	NX	*B7TL/Pres* B9TL/Gem2
172	Brockley Rise - St. Paul's	15	10	15	Abellio	WL	*Env400* Tri/ALX400

No.	Route	PVR	Freq		Operator	Garage	Type Used
173	Little Heath King George Hospital - Beckton	11	12	20	Arriva	DX	Env200
174	Harold Hill - Dagenham Marsh Way	21	8	15	Stagecoach	RM	Env400
175	Hillrise Estate - Dagenham Ford's Main Works	12	12	20	Stagecoach	NS	Tri/ALX400
176	Penge - Tottenham Court Road Station	25	8	12	Arriva	N	B7TL/ALX400 DB250/ALX400
177	Thamesmead - Peckham	18	10	12	Stagecoach	PD	N230/Omni
178	Woolwich - Lewisham	8	15	20	Stagecoach	TL	Dar/Point
179	Chingford - Ilford	10	12	20	First	DM	Env400

DN33553 based at First's Dagenham garage heads away from Chingford on route 179. *Photo: Peter Horrex*

No.	Route	PVR	Freq		Operator	Garage	Type Used
180	Thamesmead - Lewisham	14	12	20	Go-Ahead	BV	B7TL/Gem
181	Grove Park - Lewisham	11	12	15	Metrobus	MB	N94/Est
182	Harrow Weald - Brent Cross	22	8	12	Metroline	HD	B7TL/Pres Tri/Pres
183	Pinner - Golders Green	18	10	15	Lon. Sovereign	BT	B7TL/Pres B7TL/Vyk N94/Omni N230/Omni
184	Barnet - Turnpike Lane Station	17	9	12	Arriva	WN	Env200
185	Lewisham - Victoria	20	10	12	Go-Ahead	Q	B7TL/Gem B7TL/Pres
186	Northwick Park Hospital - Brent Cross	15	12	20	Metroline	EW	B7TL/Pres Env400
187	Central Middlesex Hospital - Finchley Road	14	10	15	First	WJ	Env200
188	North Greenwich - Russell Square	22	8	12	Abellio	WL	B7TL/Gem Env400H
189	Brent Cross - Oxford Circus	17	8	12	Metroline	W	Env400 Env400H
190	Richmond - West Brompton	9	15	20	Metroline	AH	E200/Evo
191	Brimsdown - Edmonton Green	16	10	15	Go-Ahead	NP	Env400

No.	Route	PVR	Freq		Operator	Garage	Type Used
192	Enfield - Edmonton Green	13	10	15	Arriva	LV	Env200
193	County Park Estate - Queen's Hospital	11	9	20	First	DM	Dar/Cap
194	Croydon - Lower Sydenham	14	12	20	Arriva	TC	*DB250/ALX400*
							DB250/Gem

Although not officially allocated, the DAF ALX400s often work on route 194. DLA185 picks-up at East Croydon station during its trip to Sydenham. *Photo: Jack Marian*

No.	Route	PVR	Freq		Operator	Garage	Type Used
195	Charville Lane - Brentford	14	12	15	First	HS	Env200
196	Norwood Junction - Elephant & Castle	14	12	20	Go-Ahead	SW	Env400
197	Croydon - Peckham	14	12	20	Arriva	TC	DB250/ALX400
							DB250/Gem
198	Shrublands - Thornton Heath	12	10	20	Arriva	TH	*DB250/ALX400*
							Env400
199	Bellingham Catford Bus Garage - Canada Water	10	12	15	Stagecoach	TL	Env400
200	Raynes Park - Mitcham	15	8	12	Go-Ahead	AL	B7TL/Pres
							Env200
							E200/Est
201	Morden - Herne Hill	9	15	20	Go-Ahead	AL	Dar/Point
							SB120/Cadet
202	Blackheath - Crystal Palace	14	10	15	Metrobus	C	Man240/Evo
203	Staines - Hounslow	6	20	30	London United	AV	Citaro
204	Edgware - Sudbury	15	10	15	Metroline	EW	Env400
205	Bow - Paddington	26	8	12	Stagecoach	BW	N230/Omni
							Tri/ALX400
206	St. Raphael's Estate - Kilburn	10	15	20	First	WJ	Env200
207	Southall - White City	35	6	8	First	HS	N230/Omni
208	Orpington - Lewisham	15	12	15	Stagecoach	TB	Tri/ALX400
209	Mortlake - Hammersmith	14	6	10	Metroline	AH	Env200
210	Brent Cross - Finsbury Park	16	8	10	Metroline	W	Env400
211	Hammersmith - Waterloo Station	19	8	12	Abellio	QB	Env400
							Env400H
212	Chingford - Walthamstow	9	10	15	CT Plus	HK	N230/Omni

No.	Route	PVR	Freq		Operator	Garage	Type Used
213	Sutton Bus Garage - Kingston	19	6	12	Go-Ahead	A	B7TL/Pres Env400 *Tri/Olym*
214	Highgate - Liverpool Street Station	18	8	12	Metroline	KC	Dar/Point
215	Yardley Lane Estate - Walthamstow	4	20	30	Stagecoach	T	N230/Omni
216	Staines - Kingston	8	20	30	London United	FW	Dar/Point Env200
217	Waltham Cross - Turnpike Lane Station	11	12	20	Metroline	PB	Tri/Pres
219	Wimbledon - Clapham Junction	11	12	15	Go-Ahead	AL	Dar/Point *E200/Est*
220	Harlesden - Wandsworth	24	8	10	London United	S	B7TL/ALX400 Tri/ALX400
221	Edgware - Turnpike Lane Station	22	12	12	Arriva	WN	B7TL/Gem *DB250/ALX400* DB250/Pres
222	Uxbridge - Hounslow	19	8	12	London United	AV	Env400
223	Harrow - South Kenton - Wembley	6	20	30	First	ON	Env200
224	Wembley Stadium Station - Willesden Junc. Station	11	15	30	First	ON	Env200
225	Hither Green - Canada Water	7	15	20	Go-Ahead	NX	Dar/Point
226	Ealing - Golders Green	15	12	20	First	WJ	Env200
227	Bromley - Crystal Palace	12	8	12	Stagecoach	TB	Citaro
228	Park Royal - Maida Hill	12	12	20	First	WJ	Env200
229	Thamesmead - Sidcup	18	10	15	Go-Ahead	BX	B9TL/Gem2 Env400
230	Upper Walthamstow - Wood Green Station	12	12	15	Stagecoach	T	Tri/ALX400
231	Enfield - Turnpike Lane Station	6	15	20	Go-Ahead	NP	Env400
232	St. Raphael's Est - Turnpike Lane Station	10	20	20	Metroline	W	Env200
233	Swanley - Eltham	6	20	30	Arriva Sth Cou.	DT	Env200
234	Barnet - East Finchley	12	10	20	Metroline	PB	Env200
235	Lower Sunbury - Brentford	19	8	12	Abellio	TF	Dar/Nimb Dar/Point
236	Hackney Wick - Finsbury Park	15	8	12	First	LI	Env200

One of Lea Interchange's new 10.8m Enviro200s, DMV44228 waits on the stand at Finsbury Park Interchange. *Photo: David McKay*

No.	Route	PVR	Freq		Operator	Garage	Type Used
237	Hounslow Heath - White City	20	8	12	Metroline	AH	B9TL/Gem2 *Tri/Pres*
238	Barking - Stratford	11	10	15	Stagecoach	WH	Env400 *Tri/ALX400*
240	Edgware - Golders Green	11	12	20	Metroline	EW	B7TL/Pres
241	Stratford City - Canning Town	10	10	20	Stagecoach	WH	Tri/ALX400
242	Homerton Hospital - Tottenham Court Road	28	6	10	Arriva	CT	B7TL/Gem DB300/Gem2 *Env400*

DW417 was one of the first batch ECWVTA specification buses in London. Here it is enters Threadneedle Street at Bank on route 242. *Photo: Peter Horrex*

No.	Route	PVR	Freq		Operator	Garage	Type Used
243	Wood Green Station - Waterloo	30	7	10	Arriva	AR	B5L/Gem2 DB250/ALX400 *DB300/Gem2*
244	Abbey Wood - Queen Elizabeth Hospital	12	10	15	Go-Ahead	BV	Env200
245	Alperton - Golders Green	21	8	12	First	ON	Env200
246	Westerham - Bromley	4	30	60	Stagecoach	TB	Env200
247	Barkingside - Romford	11	10	20	Stagecoach	NS	Tri/ALX400
248	Cranham - Romford	14	8	15	Stagecoach	RM	N230/Omni
249	Anerley Station - Clapham Common	12	12	15	Go-Ahead	AL	B9TL/Gem2
250	Croydon - Brixton	23	8	12	Arriva	TH	DB250/ALX400 Env400
251	Edgware - Arnos Grove	12	12	20	Lon. Sovereign	BT	Env200
252	Collier Row - Hornchurch	12	10	15	First	DM	Env400
253	Hackney Central Station - Euston	27	6	8	Arriva	SF	B7TL/Gem DB250/ALX400
254	Holloway Parkhurst Road - Aldgate	29	6	8	Arriva	AE	B7TL/Gem *DB250/ALX400*

No.	Route	PVR	Freq		Operator	Garage	Type Used
255	Pollards Hill - Streatham Hill	8	12	20	Arriva	TH	*Dar/Point*
							SB120/Cadet
256	Noak Hill - St. George's Hospital	10	10	20	Arriva Sth Cou.	GY	Env200
257	Walthamstow - Stratford	14	8	12	Stagecoach	WH	Tri/ALX400
258	Watford - South Harrow	11	15	30	Arriva Shires	GR	DB250/Gem
259	Edmonton Green - King's Cross	20	8	10	Go-Ahead	NP	*B7TL/Pres*
							B9TL/Gem2
							Tri/Pres
260	Golders Green - White City	16	13	15	Metroline	AC	B7TL/Pres
261	Princess Royal University Hospital - Lewisham	11	12	15	Metrobus	MB	N94/Omni
262	East Beckton - Stratford	12	10	15	Stagecoach	WH	Tri/ALX400
263	Barnet Hospital - Holloway	15	10	12	Metroline	PB	Env400
							Tri/Pres
264	Croydon - St. George's Hospital	14	10	15	Arriva	TC	DB250/Gem
265	Tolworth - Putney Bridge	11	12	15	London United	TV	Dar/Point
266	Brent Cross - Hammersmith	25	8	10	First	AS	B9TL/Gem2
267	Fulwell - Hammersmith	16	10	15	London United	FW	N94/Omni
							N230/Omni
							Tri/ALX400

SLE15 nears its destination as it passes through Fulwell. During Summer months this route is extended to Hampton Court. Photo: *Peter Horrex*

Arriva The Shires operate the short 3 mile route 268 with SB120 Cadets. *Photo: Ken Carr*

No.	Route	PVR	Freq		Operator	Garage	Type Used
268	Golders Green - Finchley Road	6	12	12	Arriva Shires	GR	SB120/Cadet
269	Bexleyheath - Bromley	14	10	15	Stagecoach	TB	Tri/ALX400
270	Mitcham - Putney Bridge	13	10	12	Go-Ahead	AL	B7TL/Gem
							B7TL/Pres
							Env400
271	Highgate - Moorgate	12	8	12	Metroline	HT	B7TL/Pres
							Tri/Pres
272	Chiswick (Grove Park) - Shepherd's Bush	8	15	15	London United	PK	Env200
273	Petts Wood - Lewisham	8	20	30	Stagecoach	TL	Dar/ALX200
							Env200
274	Lancaster Gate - Islington	17	8	8	Metroline	KC	Env200
275	Barkingside - Walthamstow St. James Street Stn.	10	12	20	Stagecoach	T	Env400
276	Stoke Newington - Newham General Hospital	19	12	15	Go-Ahead	SI	Env200
277	Highbury - Leamouth	21	7	10	Stagecoach	BW	Tri/ALX400
279	Waltham Cross - Manor House	32	6	10	Arriva	E	*B7TL/Gem*
							Env400
280	Belmont - Tooting St. George's Hospital	14	10	12	Go-Ahead	AL	Env400
281	Tolworth - Hounslow	23	8	12	London United	FW	*N94/Omni*
							N230/Omni
							Tri/ALX400
282	Mount Vernon Hospital - Ealing Hospital	16	12	15	First	G	*Env400*
							Tri/Pres
283	East Acton - Barn Elms	16	8	12	London United	PK	Versa
284	Grove Park Cemetery - Lewisham	10	12	20	Metrobus	MB	N94/Est
285	Heathrow Airport Central - Kingston	19	10	12	London United	HH	Env200
286	Sidcup - Greenwich	13	10	15	Arriva Sth Cou.	DT	Env200
287	Abbey Wood Lane - Barking	7	15	20	Stagecoach	RM	Env400

No.	Route	PVR	Freq		Operator	Garage	Type Used
288	Broadfields - Queensbury	6	10	15	Arriva Shires	GR	SB120/Cadet
289	Purley - Elmers End	10	15	20	Arriva	TH	Env200
290	Staines - Twickenham	6	20	20	Abellio	TF	Env200
291	Woodlands Estate - Queen Elizabeth Hospital	7	10	15	Stagecoach	PD	Dar/Point *Env200*
292	Borehamwood - Colindale	9	15	20	Lon. Sovereign	BT	B7TL/Pres *B7TL/Vyk N94/Omni N230/Omni*
293	Epsom General Hospital - Morden	6	20	30	Metrobus	C	N230/Omni
294	Noak Hill - Havering Park	11	12	20	Stagecoach	NS	Tri/ALX400
295	Ladbroke Grove - Clapham Junction	19	8	12	First	X	B9TL/Gem2
296	Romford - Ilford	6	20	30	Stagecoach	NS	Env200
297	Willesden Garage - Ealing Haven Green	16	10	12	Metroline	PA	B9TL/Gem2 N230/Olym
298	Potters Bar - Arnos Grove	5	20	30	Sullivan	SM	Env200
299	Cockfosters - Muswell Hill	7	15	30	Go-Ahead	NP	Env200
300	East Ham - Canning Town	9	15	20	Go-Ahead	BE	Env200
302	Mill Hill - Kensal Rise	16	8	12	Metroline	AC	B7TL/Pres
303	Colindale - Edgware	6	15	20	Arriva Shires	GR	SB120/Cadet
305	Kingsbury - Edgware	4	15	30	Arriva Shires	GR	SB120/Cadet
307	Brimsdown - Arkley Hotel	14	10	20	Arriva	E	DB250/Pres
308	Wanstead - Clapton Park Millfields	9	15	30	First	LI	Env200
309	Canning Town Station - London Chest Hospital	8	12	15	CT Plus	HK	Solo
312	South Croydon - Norwood Junction	6	12	20	Arriva	TC	Dar/Point *Env200*
313	Potters Bar - Chingford	7	20	30	Arriva	E	Env200

ENX6 from Enfield garage runs past The Green in Station Road, Chingford at the end of its journey from Potters Bar. *Photo: Peter Horrex*

No.	Route	PVR	Freq		Operator	Garage	Type Used
314	New Addington - Eltham	12	15	30	Stagecoach	TB	Env200
315	West Norwood Station - Balham	4	20	30	Go-Ahead	SW	Dar/Point
316	Cricklewood - White City	18	8	12	Metroline	W	Env200

No.	Route	PVR	Freq		Operator	Garage	Type Used
317	Waltham Cross - Enfield	5	20	30	Arriva	E	DB250/ALX400
318	North Middlesex Hospital - Stamford Hill	7	15	20	Arriva	LV	Dar/Point
319	Streatham Hill - Sloane Square	19	8	12	Arriva	BN	DB250/ALX400

Brixton's VLA155 at Streatham on route 319. This is usually operated by the DAF DB250 ALX400s. *Photo: Adam Murray*

No.	Route	PVR	Freq		Operator	Garage	Type Used
320	Biggin Hill Valley - Catford	12	12	20	Metrobus	MB	N94/Omni N230/Omni
321	Foots Cray - New Cross	19	8	12	Go-Ahead	BX/NX	B7TL/Pres
322	Crystal Palace - Clapham Common	8	15	20	Abellio	BC	Dar/Point
323	Canning Town Station - Mile End	4	15	20	Stagecoach	WH	Env200
324	Stanmore - Brent Cross	6	20	20	Lon. Sovereign BT		Env200
325	Prince Regent Station - Beckton	11	12	20	Arriva	DX	Env200
326	Barnet - Brent Cross	14	12	15	Metroline	W	Env200
327	Waltham Cross - Waltham Cross	1	30	-	Arriva	E	Dar/Point
328	Golders Green - Chelsea	27	7	10	First	AS	B7TL/Gem Gem2 HEV
329	Enfield - Turnpike Lane Station	15	7	8	Arriva	AD	DB250/Pres Env400
330	Forest Gate - Canning Town	8	12	20	Stagecoach	WH	Tri/ALX400
331	Ruislip - Uxbridge	7	20	30	First	UX	Env200
332	Neasden - Paddington	15	10	12	Metroline	W	Env400
333	Tooting - Elephant & Castle	14	10	12	Go-Ahead	SW	B7TL/Gem B7TL/Pres *Env400*
336	Locksbottom - Catford	7	20	30	Metrobus	MB	Dar/Est
337	Richmond - Clapham Junction	12	12	15	Go-Ahead	SW	Env400
339	Stratford City - Shadwell Station	6	15	20	First	LI	Env200
340	Edgware - Harrow	9	12	20	Arriva Shires	GR	DB250/ALX400
341	Lea Valley - Waterloo County Hall	21	10	12	Arriva	LV	Env400

No.	Route	PVR	Freq		Operator	Garage	Type Used
343	New Cross Gate - City Hall	23	7	10	Abellio	WL	B7TL/Gem Env400
344	Clapham Junction - Bishopsgate	23	7	10	Abellio	QB	Env400 Tri/ALX400
345	Peckham - South Kensington	25	8	10	Go-Ahead	Q	Env400
346	Upminster Park Estate - Upminster	2	15	-	Arriva Sth Cou.	GY	Dar/Point
347	Ockendon Station - Romford (10am - 4pm only)	1	120	-	Go-Ahead	BE	Env200
349	Ponders End - Stamford Hill	14	8	12	Arriva	E	B7TL/Gem DB250/ALX400 DB250/Pres

VLW101 runs along Clapton Common, Stamford Hill, shortly after starting out on its journey to Ponders End.
Photo: Madeleine Carr

No.	Route	PVR	Freq		Operator	Garage	Type Used
350	Hayes - Heathrow Airport Terminal 5	8	12	20	Abellio	WS	Tri/ALX400
352	Lower Sydenham - Bromley	5	20	-	Metrobus	MB	Dar/Point
353	Ramsden - Addington Interchange	6	15	30	Metrobus	MB	N94/Omni
354	Penge - Bromley	5	20	-	Stagecoach	TB	Env200
355	Mitcham - Brixton	12	12	15	Go-Ahead	Q	Dar/Point
356	Shirley - Upper Sydenham	6	20	30	Stagecoach	TL	Env200
357	Chingford Hatch - Whipps Cross	7	15	30	Go-Ahead	NP	B9TL/Gem2
358	Orpington Station - Crystal Palace	15	12	20	Metrobus	MB	CN94/Omni
359	Addington Interchange - Selsdon (10am - 3pm only)	1	35	-	Metrobus	C	Man240/Env200
360	Kensington - Elephant & Castle	11	12	15	Go-Ahead	Q	Dar/Point SB120/Ecity Versa Hybrid
362	Grange Hill - Little Heath King George Hospital	3	30	30	Go-Ahead	BE	Env200
363	Crystal Palace - Elephant & Castle	12	10	15	Go-Ahead	PM	B7TL/Pres B9TL/Gem2 Env400
364	Dagenham East - Ilford	13	10	15	Go-Ahead	BE	Env200
365	Mardyke Estate - Havering Park	10	12	20	First	DM	Env400

No.	Route	PVR	Freq		Operator	Garage	Type Used
366	Redbridge - Beckton	15	12	20	Stagecoach	BK	Env200
367	Bromley - Croydon	9	20	30	Metrobus	MB	Dar/Est
368	Chadwell Heath - Harts Lane Estate	7	12	20	First	DM	Env200
370	Lakeside - Romford	10	15	30	Arriva Sth Cou.	GY	DB250/ALX400 Env200
371	Kingston - Richmond	15	9	12	London United	FW	*Dar/Point* Env200 Env200H Tri/ALX400

HDE5 stops in Eden Street, Kingston. It is one of London United's five Hybrid Enviro200s based at Fulwell to work on route 371. *Photo: Adam Murray*

No.	Route	PVR	Freq		Operator	Garage	Type Used
372	Lakeside - Hornchurch	6	20	30	Stagecoach	RM	Env200 Env400
375	Passingford Bridge - Romford	1	90	-	Arriva Sth Cou.	GY	Env200
376	Beckton - East Ham	8	15	30	Go-Ahead	BE	Env200
377	Oakwood - Ponders End	3	30	-	Arriva	E	Dar/Point
379	Yardley Lane Estate - Chingford	2	15	30	Arriva	LV	Env200
380	Belmarsh - Lewisham	12	12	15	Stagecoach	TL	Dar/ALX200 Dar/Point Tempo Hybrid
381	Peckham - Waterloo County Hall	17	11	12	Abellio	WL	B7TL/Gem
382	Mill Hill East - Southgate	8	15	30	Arriva	WN	Dar/Point
383	Barnet - Woodside Park Station	3	30	-	Metroline	PB	Env200
384	Quinta Drive - Cockfosters	8	15	30	Metroline	PB	Env200
385	Chingford - Crooked Billet (10am - 3pm only)	1	60	-	CT Plus	HK	Dar/Point
386	Woolwich - Blackheath Village	10	15	20	Stagecoach	PD	*Dar/Point* Env200
387	Little Heath - Barking Reach	10	12	20	Stagecoach	BK	Env400

CT Plus's Trident Lolyne HTL6 at Bank shortly after starting its journey to Hackney Wick. *Photo: Ken Carr*

No.	Route	PVR	Freq		Operator	Garage	Type Used
388	Hackney Wick - Blackfriars	11	10	12	CT Plus	HK	Tri/Loly
							Tri/Olym
389	Barnet - Barnet Salisbury Road (11am - 4pm only)	1	60	-	Go-Ahead	NP	Env200
390	Archway - Notting Hill Gate	20	8	12	Metroline	HT	B7TL/Pres
391	Richmond - Sands End	18	10	12	London United	V	Versa
393	Clapton - Chalk Farm	14	12	20	Arriva	AE/ CT	Env200
							Env200
394	Homerton Hospital - Islington	10	12	20	CT Plus	HK	Dar/Nimb
							Env200
395	Westway Cross - Harrow	4	22	30	Metroline	PA	Env200
396	Little Heath King George Hospital - Ilford	5	20	20	Stagecoach	BK	Versa
397	Debden - Crooked Billet	5	30	30	Arriva	LV	Env200
398	Ruislip - Wood End	3	30	-	Lon.Sovereign	SO	Dar/Point
							Env200
399	Barnet - Barnet (10am - 3pm only)	1	60	-	Go-Ahead	NP	Env200
401	Thamesmead - Bexleyheath	7	15	30	Go-Ahead	BX	B7TL/Pres
							B9TL/Gem
403	Warlingham - Croydon	8	12	20	Arriva	TC	DB250/Gem
404	Caterham-on-the-Hill - Coulsdon	1	60	-	Quality Line	EB	Solo
405	Redhill - Croydon	9	15	30	Metrobus	C	N230/Omni
406	Epsom - Kingston	4	30	30	Quality Line	EB	Env400
407	Caterham - Sutton	13	15	20	Abellio	BC	Tri/ALX400
							Env200
410	Wallington - Crystal Palace	19	9	15	Arriva	TH	Dar/Point
							SB120/Cadet
411	West Molesey - Kingston	6	20	30	Quality Line	EB	Versa
412	Purley - Croydon	8	15	20	Arriva	TC	DB250/ALX400
							DB250/Gem
413	Sutton - Morden	7	15	30	Go-Ahead	A	Dar/Point
							E200/Est

No.	Route	PVR	Freq		Operator	Garage	Type Used
414	Putney Bridge Station - Maida Hill	18	8	12	Abellio	QB	Env400
415	Tulse Hill - Elephant & Castle	7	12	20	Arriva	N	B7TL/ALX400
							DB250/ALX400
417	Crystal Palace - Clapham Common	11	10	15	Arriva	N	B7TL/ALX400
418	Epsom - Kingston	4	30	30	Quality Line	EB	Env400
419	Richmond - Hammersmith	7	15	30	London United	NC	Dar/Point
422	Bexleyheath Bus Garage - North Greenwich	16	10	20	Go-Ahead	BX	B9TL/Gem2
							Env400
423	Heathrow Airport (Terminal 5) - Hounslow	7	20	30	London United	HH	Env200
424	Putney Heath - Fulham Craven Cottage	5	30	-	Go-Ahead	AF	Dar/Point
425	Clapton Nightingale Road - Stratford	9	12	15	Go-Ahead	SI	*B9TL/Gem2*
							B9TL/MCV
							N94/Omni
							N230/Omni
427	Uxbridge - Acton	22	8	10	First	HS	B9TL/Gem2

One of Hayes garage's Gemini 2s, VN37871 heads through Ealing Common. *Photo: Peter Horrex*

No.	Route	PVR	Freq		Operator	Garage	Type Used
428	Bluewater - Erith	8	15	30	Arriva Sth Cou.	DT	Env200
430	Roehampton - South Kensington	15	8	10	Go-Ahead	AF	B7TL/Gem
432	Anerley Station - Brixton	9	12	15	Arriva	N	B7TL/ALX400
							DB250/ALX400
434	Rickman Hill - Whyteleafe Station	3	30	-	Abellio	BC	Env200
436	Lewisham - Paddington	32	8	12	Go-Ahead	NX	Env400
							Env400H

No.	Route	PVR	Freq		Operator	Garage	Type Used
440	Stonebridge Park Station - Gunnersbury	10	15	20	London United	PK	Env200
444	Chingford - Turnpike Lane Station	8	15	20	Arriva	LV	*Dar/Point*
							SB120/Cadet
450	Lower Sydenham - West Croydon	13	12	20	Arriva	TH	Dar/Point
452	Kensal Rise - Wandsworth Road Station	20	8	12	Abellio	QB	Env400
453	Deptford - Marylebone Station	34	8	10	Go-Ahead	MW	Env400
455	Old Lodge Lane - Wallington	10	20	30	Abellio	BC	Dar/Nimb
460	North Finchley - Willesden	11	13	15	Metroline	AC	B7TL/Pres
462	Hainault - Ilford	8	15	30	Go-Ahead	BE	Street

Wheel-forward StreetLite WS6 works the 462 through Grange Hill. *Photo: Peter Horrex*

No.	Route	PVR	Freq		Operator	Garage	Type Used
463	Coulsdon South Station - Pollards Hill	8	20	30	Quality Line	EB	Solo
464	Tatsfield - New Addington	3	30	60	Metrobus	MB	Dar/Point
465	Dorking - Kingston	5	30	60	Quality Line	EB	Versa
466	Caterham-on-the-Hill - Addington Interchange	18	10	15	Arriva	TC	*DB250/ALX400*
							DB250/Gem
							Env400
467	Hook - Epsom	2	60	-	Quality Line	EB	Env400
468	South Croydon - Elephant & Castle	26	8	12	Go-Ahead	Q	B7TL/Gem
							B7TL/Pres
469	Erith - Queen Elizabeth Hospital	8	15	20	Stagecoach	PD	Env200
470	Epsom - Colliers Wood	7	30	-	Quality Line	EB	Solo
472	Thamesmead - North Greenwich	20	6	10	Stagecoach	PD	Tri/ALX400
473	North Woolwich - Stratford	10	10	15	Stagecoach	WH	Tri/ALX400
474	Manor Park - Canning Town	12	12	15	Go-Ahead	SI	B9TL/Gem2
							B9TL/MCV
							N94/Omni
							N230/Omni
476	Northumberland Park - Euston	21	8	12	Go-Ahead	NP	*B7TL/Pres*
							B9TL/Gem2
							Tri/Pres

No.	Route	PVR	Freq		Operator	Garage	Type Used
481	Isleworth West Middlesex Hospital - Kingston	2	60	-	Abellio	TF	*Dar/Point* Env200
482	Southall - Heathrow Airport Terminal 5	8	20	30	London United	HH	Env400H N230/Omni
484	Lewisham - Camberwell	12	10	15	Abellio	WL	Env200
485	Wandsworth - Hammersmith	3	30	-	Go-Ahead	PL	Dar/Point
486	Bexleyheath - North Greenwich	16	8	12	Go-Ahead	BX	Env400
487	South Harrow - Willesden Junction Station	9	15	20	First	ON	Env200
488	Clapton - Bromley-by-Bow	9	12	15	Stagecoach	WH	Env200
490	Heathrow Airport Terminal 5 - Richmond	14	12	20	Abellio	TF	Env200
491	Waltham Cross - North Middlesex Hospital	10	15	30	Arriva	E	Env200

In June 2013, route 491 will be taken over by Go-Ahead with brand new single-deckers. *Photo: Peter Horrex*

No.	Route	PVR	Freq		Operator	Garage	Type Used
492	Bluewater - Sidcup	6	30	30	Arriva Sth Cou.	DT	DB250/Gem *Env400*
493	Richmond - Tooting St. George's Hospital	17	12	20	Go-Ahead	PL	Env200
496	Harold Wood - Romford	8	15	20	Stagecoach	NS	Env400 *Tri/ALX400*
498	Brentwood - Romford	3	30	60	First	DM	Env200
499	Gallows Corner - Heath Park Estate	4	30	30	Arriva Sth Cou.	GY	Env200 SB120/Cadet
507	Victoria - Waterloo	15	6	12	Go-Ahead	RA	Citaro
521	Waterloo - London Bridge (Mon-Fri only)	31	5	-	Go-Ahead	MW/RA	Citaro
549	Loughton Station - South Woodford	1	60	-	Go-Ahead	SI	Env200/Evo
603	Muswell Hill - Swiss Cottage (Mon-Fri only 4 Trips)	2			Metroline	HT	Tri/Pres
607	Uxbridge - White City	20	10	12	First	UX	B7TL/Gem Env400
A10	Uxbridge - Heathrow Airport Central	5	15	30	First	UX	Env200
B11	Thamesmead - Bexleyheath Bus Garage	7	15	30	Go-Ahead	BX	Env200
B12	Joydens Wood - Erith	6	20	-	Arriva Sth Cou.	DT	Env200
B13	New Eltham - Bexleyheath	6	15	30	Arriva Sth Cou.	DT	SB120/Cadet
B14	Orpington - Bexleyheath	5	30	30	Metrobus	MB	Env200
B15	Bexleyheath - Horn Park	5	20	30	Arriva Sth Cou.	DT	SB120/Cadet

No.	Route	PVR	Freq		Operator	Garage	Type Used
B16	Kidbrooke Station - Bexleyheath Bus Garage	8	15	30	Go-Ahead	BX	Env200
C1	White City - Victoria	14	10	12	London United	PK	Env200
C2	Parliament Hill - Victoria	19	8	10	Abellio	QB	Env400
C3	Clapham Junction - Earl's Court	12	8	12	Abellio	QB	Tri/ALX400
C10	Canada Water - Victoria	14	12	20	Abellio	QB	Env200
C11	Brent Cross - Archway	20	8	12	Metroline	W	*Dar/Point* Env200
D3	Crossharbour - Bethnal Green	15	10	15	Stagecoach	WH	Env200
D6	Crossharbour - Hackney	16	8	15	Go-Ahead	SI	Env200
D7	Poplar - Mile End	11	8	15	Go-Ahead	SI	B9TL/Gem2
D8	Crossharbour - Stratford City	8	12	20	Go-Ahead	SI	Env200
E1	Greenford - Ealing Haven Green	7	10	10	First	G	Env400
E2	Greenford - Brentford	15	8	12	Metroline	AH	B9TL/Gem2
E3	Greenford - Chiswick	26	7	10	First	G	Env400
E5	Toplocks - Perivale	11	12	20	First	G	Env200
E6	Greenford Station - Bulls Bridge	12	10	15	Metroline	PA	MAN240/Evo
E7	Ruislip - Ealing	10	12	20	First	G	Env200
E8	Brentford - Ealing	11	8	10	Metroline	AH	Env200 *E200/Evo* Temp Hybrid Tri/Pres
E9	Yeading Barnhill Estate - Ealing	8	12	20	First	G	Env200
E10	Islip Manor - Ealing	7	15	20	First	G	Env200
E11	Greenford - Ealing Common	5	20	30	London United	PK	Env200
EL1	Thames View Estate - Ilford Hill	7	12	20	Go-Ahead	BE	B9TL/Gem2

Plans for an East London tram system have been cancelled in favour of buses which operate routes EL1 & EL2. *Photo: Peter Horrex.*

EL2	Dagenham Dock - Ilford Hill	7	12	20	Go-Ahead	BE	B9TL/Gem2
G1	Streatham High Road - Shaftesbury Estate	9	20	30	Go-Ahead	PL	Dar/Point
H2	Golders Green - Golders Green (circular Trip)	3	12	15	Arriva Shires	GR	Solo
H3	Golders Green - Golders Green (circular Trip)	1	60	-	Arriva Shires	GR	Solo
H9	Harrow - Harrow (circular Trip)	8	10	20	Lon. Sovereign	SO	Dar/Point Env200

No.	Route	PVR	Freq		Operator	Garage	Type Used
H10	Harrow - Harrow (circular Trip)	7	10	20	Lon. Sovereign	SO	*Dar/Point* Env200
H11	Mount Vernon Hospital - Harrow	6	15	20	Lon. Sovereign	SO	Env200
H12	Stanmore - South Harrow	12	10	15	Metroline	HD	B7TL/Pres
H13	St. Vincent's Park - Ruislip Lido	5	20	30	Lon. Sovereign	SO	*Dar/Point* Env200
H14	Hatch End - Northwick Park Hospital	7	10	15	Lon. Sovereign	SO	*Dar/Point* Env200
H17	Wembley - Harrow	7	15	20	Lon. Sovereign	SO	Env200
H18	Harrow - Harrow (circular Trip - buses shared with H19)	5	30	30	Arriva Shires	GR	B6BLE/Crus Dar/Point SB120/Cadet
H19	Harrow - Harrow (circular Trip - buses shared with H18)	5	30	30	Arriva Shires	GR	B6BLE/Crus Dar/Point *SB120/Cadet*
H20	Ivybridge - Hounslow Civic Centre	5	12	20	Abellio	TF	Dar/Point
H22	Hounslow - Richmond	11	12	20	London United	HH	Dar/Point
H25	Butts Farm - Hatton Cross	7	15	20	Abellio	TF	Dar/Nimb
H26	Sparrow Farm - Hatton Cross	4	20	30	Abellio	TF	Env200
H28	Bulls Bridge - Osterley	8	20	30	Abellio	WS	Dar/Point
H32	Southall - Hounslow	12	10	15	London United	AV	*B7TL/ALX400* B7TL/Pres N230/Omni

A rarity in London is the centre-staircase ALX400, VA80 is one such bus, it waits on the stand at Hounslow.
Photo: Jack Marian

| H37 | Hounslow - Richmond | 15 | 6 | 8 | London United | AV | *Dar/Point*
Tempo |

No.	Route	PVR	Freq		Operator	Garage	Type Used
H91	Hounslow West - Hammersmith	14	10	15	London United	HH	N230/Omni
H98	Hayes End - Hounslow	15	8	15	London United	AV	Env200
K1	New Malden - Kingston	9	15	20	London United	TV	Env200
K2	Hook Library - Kingston Hospital	10	11	15	London United	TV	Dar/Point
K3	Esher - Roehampton Vale	11	15	30	London United	TV	Dar/Point
K4	Mansfield Estate - Kingston Hospital	4	30	-	London United	TV	Dar/Point
K5	Ham - Morden	3	60	-	Quality Line	EB	Solo
P4	Lewisham - Brixton	10	12	12	Stagecoach	TL	Dar/Point
P5	Nine Elms - Elephant & Castle	8	15	20	Go-Ahead	Q	Env200
P12	Brockley Rise - Surrey Quays	12	10	20	Go-Ahead	PM	Env200
P13	Streatham - New Cross Gate	8	20	30	Abellio	BC	Dar/Point
R1	Green Street Green - Grovelands	7	15	30	Metrobus	MB	*Dar/Point Env200*

The R1 - R11 series of routes operate in and around Orpington. Metrobus's Single-door Pointer 273 works R1 along the northern end of the High Street. *Photo: Mark Jiggins*

No.	Route	PVR	Freq		Operator	Garage	Type Used
R2	Melody Road - Petts Wood Station	4	30	-	Metrobus	MB	Man240/Est
R3	Chelsfield Village - Princess Royal University Hospital	4	30	60	Metrobus	MB	Dar/Point
R4	Pauls Cray Hill - Princess Royal University Hospital	6	20	60	Metrobus	MB	Dar/Point Env200
R5	Orpington - Orpington (circ. Trip - buses shared with R10)	1	120	-	Metrobus	MB	Dar/Point
R6	Orpington - St Mary Cray	2	30	60	Metrobus	MB	Dar/Point
R7	Orpington - Bickley	1	60	-	Metrobus	MB	Dar/Point
R8	Orpington - Biggin Hill	2	70	-	Metrobus	MB	Solo
R9	Orpington - Orpington (circular Trip)	3	12	30	Metrobus	MB	Env200
R10	Orpington - Orpington (circ. Trip - buses shared with R5)	1	120	-	Metrobus	MB	Dar/Point
R11	Green Street Green - Sidcup Queen Mary's Hospital	7	15	30	Metrobus	MB	Env200

No.	Route	PVR	Freq		Operator	Garage	Type Used
R68	Hampton Court - Kew	10	15	15	Abellio	TF	Env200
R70	Manor Circus - Nurserylands	11	10	20	Abellio	TF	Env200 SB120/Elec

Abellio's five Electrocitys now work route R70, they are joined on the route by Enviro200s. *Photo: Peter Horrex*

No.	Route	PVR	Freq		Operator	Garage	Type Used
RV1	Tower Gateway Station - Covent Garden	8	10	20	First	LI	Env200 HYDRO
S1	Banstead - Mitcham	8	20	30	Quality Line	EB	E200/Est
S3	Sutton Hospital - Malden Manor Station	8	20	-	Quality Line	EB	Dar/ALX200 Dar/Myl Env200
S4	Roundshaw - St. Helier Station	5	30	-	Quality Line	EB	E200/Est Solo
T31	New Addington - Forestdale	9	8	15	Arriva	TC	Dar/Point Env200
T32	New Addington - Addington Interchange	3	15	30	Metrobus	C	Man240/Env200
T33	Addington Interchange - Croydon	10	8	15	Abellio	BC	Env200
U1	West Drayton - Ruislip	8	15	30	First	UX	Dar/Nimb Env200
U2	Brunel University - Uxbridge	8	10	20	First	UX	Dar/Nimb Env200
U3	Heathrow Airport Central - Uxbridge	11	12	20	First	UX	Dar/Nimb Env200 Tri/Pres

No.	Route	PVR	Freq		Operator	Garage	Type Used
U4	Hayes - Uxbridge	14	8	20	First	UX	Tri/Pres
U5	Hayes - Uxbridge	11	12	20	First	UX	*Dar/Nimb* Env200
U7	Hayes - Uxbridge	4	30	30	Abellio	WS	Dar/Nimb *Dar/Point*
U9	Harefield Hospital - Uxbridge	3	20	60	Abellio	WS	Dar/Point
U10	Heathfield Rise - Uxbridge	2	60	-	First	UX	*Dar/Nimb* Env200
W3	Northumberland Park - Finsbury Park	20	6	10	Arriva	LV	Env400
W4	Oakthorpe Park - Ferry Lane Estate	11	10	15	Go-Ahead	NP	Env200
W5	Archway - Harringay	7	12	20	CT Plus	HK	Solo
W6	Southgate - Edmonton Green	8	10	15	Arriva	LV	Dar/Point
W7	Muswell Hill - Finsbury Park	16	6	8	Metroline	HT	B9TL/Gem2
W8	Chase Farm Hospital - Picketts Lock	14	8	12	Metroline	PB	Tri/Pres
W9	Chase Farm Hospital - Southgate	8	15	30	Metroline	PB	Dar/Point Env200
W10	Crews Hill - Enfield (11am-3pm)	1	60	-	Go-Ahead	NP	Dar/Cap
W11	Chingford Hall Estate - Walthamstow	7	10	15	Arriva	LV	Env200
W12	Wanstead - Coppermill Lane	6	20	30	CT Plus	HK	Solo
W13	Woodford Wells - Leytonstone	5	15	30	CT Plus	HK	E200/Est
W14	Woodford Bridge - Leyton	10	15	20	First	LI	Env200
W15	Cogan Avenue - Hackney	20	8	12	First	LI	Env200
W16	Chingford Mount - Leytonstone Station	8	12	20	Go-Ahead	NP	Env200
W19	Ilford - Walthamstow	8	20	30	Go-Ahead	BE	Dar/Evo
X26	West Croydon - Heathrow Airport Central	9	30	30	Quality Line	EB	Citaro
X68	West Croydon - Russell Square (Mon-Fri peak hours)	7	20	-	Go-Ahead	Q PM	B7TL/Gem B7TL/Pres

The limited stop X68 only operates Monday to Friday during peak hours. WVL226 sets down at Croydon.
Photo: Adam Murray

Night Buses

No.	Route	PVR	Freq mf	sat	Operator	Garage	Type Used
N1	Thamesmead - Tottenham Court Road	9	30	20	Go-Ahead	BV	B7TL/Gem
						MW	B7TL/Gem
N2	Crystal Palace - Trafalgar Square	5	30	20	Arriva	N	B7TL/ALX400
							Env400
N3	Bromley - Oxford Circus	13	30	15	Abellio	QB	Env400H
N5	Edgware - Trafalgar Square	17	15	10	Metroline	EW	B7TL/Pres
							Env400
						HT	B7TL/Pres
6	Willesden Garage - Aldwych	10	15	12	Metroline	AC	B7TL/Pres
N7	Northolt - Russell Square	7	30	30	Metroline	PA	N230/Olym
N8	Hainault - Oxford Circus	23	20	8	Stagecoach	BW	Tri/ALX400
N9	Heathrow Airport Terminal 5 - Aldwych	17	20	10	London United	AV	B7TL/ALX400
							B7TL/Pres
							N230/Omni

The N9 differs from the daytime route 9. The night service is extended from Hammersmith to Heathrow Airport. Different garages also supply buses for the two routes, the 9 is operated by Stamford Brook garage, whereas N9 is operated by Hounslow. SP166 picks-up at Hammersmith bus station. *Photo: Jack Marian*

10	Hammersmith - King's Cross	4	30	30	London United	V	N230/Omni
N11	Ealing - Liverpool Street	7	30	30	Go-Ahead	SW	B7TL/Gem

No.	Route	PVR	Freq mf	sat	Operator	Garage	Type Used
12	Dulwich Library - Oxford Circus	8	30	15	Go-Ahead	Q	B5LH/Gem2 B9TL/Gem2
N13	North Finchley - Aldwych	10	30	15	Lon.Sovereign	BT	N94/Omni N230/Omni
14	Putney Heath - University College Hospital	13	15	10	Go-Ahead	AF	B7TL/Gem
N15	Romford - Piccadilly Circus	14	15	10	Stagecoach	BK	Env400 Tri/ALX400
N16	Edgware - Victoria	7	20	20	Metroline	W	B7TL/Pres Env400
						HD	B7TL/Pres
N18	Harrow Weald - Trafalgar Square	15	15	10	First	WJ	B9TL/Gem2
N19	Clapham Junction - Finsbury Park	8	30	20	Go-Ahead	SW	B5LH/Gem2 B9TL/Gem2
N20	Barnet - Trafalgar Square	14	30	12	Metroline	HT	Tri/Pres
						PB	Tri/Pres
N21	Bexleyheath - Trafalgar Square	5	30	30	Go-Ahead	NX	B7TL/Pres B9TL/Gem2
						BX	B9TL/Gem2 Env400
N22	Fulwell - Piccadilly Circus	8	30	20	Go-Ahead	AF	B7TL/Gem
23	Westbourne Park - Liverpool Street	5	30	30	First	X	B9TL/Gem2 Env400H
24	Hampstead Heath - Pimlico	8	15	15	Go-Ahead	SW	Env400
25	Ilford - Oxford Circus	29	8	6	First	LI	B9TL/Gem2
N26	Chingford - Trafalgar Square	8	20	20	First	LI	Tri/ALX400
27	Turnham Green - Camden Town	4	30	30	London United	AV	B7TL/ALX400 B7TL/Pres N230/Omni
N28	Wandsworth - Camden Town	4	60	30	First	AS	B7TL/Gem
N29	Enfield - Trafalgar Square	37	8	4	Arriva	WN	DB300/GEM2
N31	Clapham Junction - Camden Town	4	60	30	First	AS	B7TL/Gem
33	Fulwell - Hammersmith	3	30	30	London United	NC	Dar/Point
N35	Clapham Junction - Tottenham Court Road Station	12	30	12	Abellio	WL	Env400
36	New Cross Gate - Queens Park	6	20	30	Go-Ahead	PM	B7TL/Pres
37	Putney Heath - Peckham	4	30	30	Go-Ahead	PM	Env400
N38	Walthamstow - Victoria	26	12	12	Arriva	CT	DB250/ALX400
N41	Tottenham Hale - Trafalgar Square	5	30	30	Arriva	AR	DB300/Gem2
43	Friern Barnet - London Bridge	6	30	20	Metroline	HT	Tri/Pres
N44	Sutton - Aldwych	9	30	20	Go-Ahead	SW	B7TL/Gem B7TL/Pres
N47	St. Mary Cray Station - Trafalgar Square	10	30	20	Stagecoach	TL	Tri/ALX400
N52	Willesden - Victoria	4	30	30	Metroline	AC	B7TL/Pres
53	Plumstead Station - Whitehall	7	20	20	Stagecoach	PD	Env400 N230/Omni
N55	Woodford Wells - Oxford Circus	11	30	15	Stagecoach	T	Tri/ALX400
57	Kingston - Clapham Park	4	30	30	London United	TV	Tri/ALX400
N63	Crystal Palace - King's Cross	8	30	15	Go-Ahead	PM	B9TL/Gem2
N64	Homestead Way - Thornton Heath Bus Garage	3	30	30	Metrobus	C	N230/Omni
65	Chessington World of Adventures - Ealing	4	30	30	London United	FW	N230/Omni
N68	Camberwell - Tottenham Court Road Station	6	30	30	Go-Ahead	Q	B9TL/Gem2
69	Walthamstow - Canning Town	3	30	30	Stagecoach	T	Tri/ALX400
72	Roehampton - East Acton	3	30	30	London United	S	Env200
N73	Walthamstow - Victoria	13	30	12	Arriva	SF	Gem2Int B5L/Gem2
N74	Danebury Avenue - Baker Street	5	30	30	Go-Ahead	AF	B7TL/Gem
N76	Northumberland Park - Waterloo	5	30	30	Arriva	AR	B5TL/Gem B7TL/ALX400

No.	Route	PVR	Freq mf	sat	Operator	Garage	Type Used
83	Ealing Hospital - Golders Green	4	30	30	First	ON	B9TL/Gem2
85	Kingston - Putney	3	30	30	Go-Ahead	AF	B7TL/Gem B9TL/Env400
N86	Dagnam Park Drive - Stratford	5	30	30	Stagecoach	NS	Tri/ALX400
N87	Kingston - Aldwych	16	15	10	Go-Ahead	SW	B7TL/Gem B7TL/Pres
88	Clapham Common - Camden Town	7	30	20	Go-Ahead	SW	B7TL/Gem B7TL/Pres
N89	Erith - Trafalgar Square	10	30	20	Go-Ahead	BX	B9TL/Gem2 Env400
N91	Cockfosters - Trafalgar Square	14	30	15	Metroline	HT PB	Env400 Env400
93	North Cheam - Putney	3	30	30	Go-Ahead	A	Tri/Olym
94	Acton Green - Piccadilly Circus	6	30	15	London United	S	Env400H Tri/ALX400
N97	Hammersmith - Trafalgar Square	9	20	10	London United	S	B7TL/ALX400 N230/Omni

Route N97 is totally different to the daytime route 97 which is operated by Stagecoach in East London. The N97, operated by London United, runs from Hammersmith to Trafalgar Square. Shepherd's Bush garage's SP124 awaits its first trip of the night at Hammersmith bus station. *Photo: Jack Marian*

No.	Route	PVR	Freq mf	sat	Operator	Garage	Type Used
N98	Stanmore - Holborn	13	15	10	Metroline	EW	B7TL/Pres
							Env400
						AC	B7TL/Pres
102	Edmonton Green - Golders Green	4	30	30	Arriva	AD	Env400
105	Greenford Station - Heathrow Airport Central	3	30	30	Metroline	PA	B9TL/Gem2
108	Lewisham - Stratford	4	30	30	Go-Ahead	NX	SB120/Cadet
N109	Croydon - Oxford Circus	9	20	20	Arriva	BN	DB250/ALX400
111	Heathrow Airport Central - Kingston	23	30	30	London United	AV	N230/Omni
N113	Mitcham - Trafalgar Square	5	30	30	Metroline	EW	B7TL/Pres
119	Bromley - Purley Way	3	30	30	Metrobus	MB	N94/Omni
128	Claybury - Romford	5	30	30	Arriva	DX	B7TL/ALX400
N133	Mitcham - Liverpool Street Station	6	20	20	Arriva	TC	Env400
134	North Finchley - Tottenham Court Road	10	15	12	Metroline	HT	B9TL/Gem2
N136	Chislehurst War Memorial - Oxford Circus	10	30	20	Stagecoach	TL	Tri/ALX400
N137	Crystal Palace - Oxford Circus	10	30	15	Arriva	N	Env400
139	West Hampstead - Waterloo	4	30	30	Metroline	W	Env400H
140	Harrow Weald - Heathrow Airport Central	4	30	30	Metroline	HD	B7TL/Pres
148	Denmark Hill - White City	6	20	20	London United	S	B7TL/ALX400
							N230/Omni
149	Edmonton Green - London Bridge	4	30	30	Arriva	AR	DB300/Gem2
N155	Morden -Aldwych	19	15	8	Go-Ahead	AL	B7TL/Gem
							B7TL/Pres
						A	Tri/Olym
159	Streatham - Paddington Basin	8	20	20	Arriva	BN	B7TL/ALX400
							DB300/Gem2
N171	Hither Green - Tottenham Court Road	5	30	30	Go-Ahead	NX	B9TL/Gem2
176	Penge - Tottenham Court Road Station	9	30	20	Arriva	N	B7TL/ALX400
							DB250/ALX400
188	North Greenwich - Russell Square	4	30	30	Abellio	WL	Env400H
189	Brent Cross - Oxford Circus	4	30	30	Metroline	W	Env400H
205	Bow - Paddington	5	30	30	Stagecoach	BW	N230/Omni
							Tri/ALX400
N207	Uxbridge - Holborn	21	15	8	First	HS	N94/Omni
213	Sutton Bus Garage - Kingston	3	30	30	Go-Ahead	A	B7TL/Pres
214	Highgate - Liverpool Street Station	9	20	10	Metroline	KC	Dar/Point
220	Harlesden - Wandsworth	3	30	30	London United	S	Env400H
236	Hackney Wick - Finsbury Park	3	30	30	First	LI	Env200
238	Barking - Stratford	3	20	20	Stagecoach	WH	Env400
242	Homerton Hospital - Tottenham Court Road	9	20	15	Arriva	CT	B7TL/Gem
							DB300/Gem2
243	Wood Green Station - Waterloo	5	30	30	Arriva	AR	B5L/Gem2
							DB250/ALX400
							DB300/Gem2
250	Croydon - Brixton	4	30	30	Arriva	TH	DB250/ALX400
							Env400
N253	Aldgate - Tottenham Court Road Station	13	15	12	Arriva	SF	B7TL/Gem
264	Croydon - St. George's Hospital	3	30	30	Arriva	TC	DB250/Gem
266	Brent Cross - Hammersmith	4	30	30	First	AS	B9TL/Gem2
271	Highgate - Moorgate	2	30	30	Metroline	HT	Tri/Pres
277	Highbury - Leamouth	3	30	30	Stagecoach	WH	Tri/ALX400
N279	Waltham Cross - Trafalgar Square	15	20	12	Arriva	E	B7TL/Gem
							Env400
281	Tolworth - Hounslow	4	30	30	London United	FW	Tri/ALX400
285	Heathrow Airport Central - Kingston	4	30	30	London United	HH	Env200
295	Ladbroke Grove - Clapham Junction	4	30	30	First	X	B9TL/Gem2
							Tri/Pres
297	Willesden Garage - Ealing Haven Green	4	30	30	Metroline	PA	Env400
321	Foots Cray - New Cross	3	30	30	Go-Ahead	NX	B7TL/Pres

147

No.	Route	PVR	Freq mf	sat	Operator	Garage	Type Used
341	Lea Valley - Waterloo County Hall	4	30	30	Arriva	LV	Env400
N343	New Cross Gate - Trafalgar Square	5	30	30	Abellio	WL	B7TL/Gem Env400
344	Clapham Junction - Bishopsgate	4	30	30	Abellio	QB	Env400
345	Peckham - South Kensington	4	30	30	Go-Ahead	Q	Env400
365	Mardyke Estate - Havering Park	3	30	30	First	DM	Env400
N381	Peckham - Trafalgar Square	4	30	30	Abellio	WL	B7TL/Gem
390	Archway - Notting Hill Gate	4	30	30	Metroline	HT	B7TL/Pres
453	Deptford - Marylebone Station	11	20	12	Go-Ahead	MW	Env400
472	Thamesmead - North Greenwich	3	30	30	Stagecoach	PD	N230/Omni Tri/ALX400
474	Manor Park - Canning Town	3	30	30	Go-Ahead	SI	N94/Omni
N550	Canning Town - Trafalgar Square	5	30	30	Stagecoach	WH	Tri/ALX400
N551	Gallions Reach - Trafalgar Square	6	30	30	Go-Ahead	SI	N94/Omni
C2	Parliament Hill - Victoria	4	30	30	Abellio	QB	Env400
EL1	Thames View Estate - Ilford Hill	2	30	30	Go-Ahead	BE	B9TL/Gem2

School Buses

No.	Route	Operator	Garage	Type Used
601	Thamesmead - Dartford Heath	Stagecoach	PD	Tri/ALX400
602	Thamesmead - Bexleyheath Grammar School	Stagecoach	PD	Tri/ALX400
605	Edgware - Mill Hill County School	Lon.Sovereign	BT	B7TL/Pres
606	Queensbury - Ravenscroft School	Metroline	EW	B7TL/Pres Env400
608	Gallows Corner - Shenfield High School	First	DM	B7TL/Gem
609	Hammersmith - Harrodian School	Metroline	AH	Env200
611	Stonebridge Park - East Finchley Cemetery	Metroline	PA	N230/Olym Tri/Pres
612	Sanderstead - Wallington County Grammar School	Metrobus	C	N230/Omni N94/Omni
613	Worcester Park - Glenthorne High School	London United	TV	Tri/ALX400
616	Green Dragon Lane - Edmonton Green	Go-Ahead	NP	Tri/Pres
617	Turnpike Lane Station - St. Ignatius College	Arriva	WN	DB250/ALX400
621	Lewisham - Crown Woods School	Go-Ahead	NX	B7TL/Pres
624	Grove Park - Crown Woods School	Go-Ahead	MW	B7TL/Gem Env400
625	Plumstead Common - Chislehurst	Go-Ahead	BX	B7TL/Gem
626	Finchley - Potters Bar Dame Alice Owen's School	Metroline	PB	Tri/Pres
627	Worcester Park - Wallington High School	Arriva	TC	DB250/Gem
628	Kingsbury - Southgate	Sullivans	SM	Tri/ALX400
629	Wood Green Station - St. Ignatius College	Arriva	AD	DB250/Pres Env400
632	Kilburn Park - Grahame Park Corner Mead	Metroline	W	Tri/Pres
634	Muswell Hill - Barnet Hospital	Arriva	AD	DB250/Pres Env400
635	Brentford - Sunbury St. Paul's School	Metroline	AH	Tri/Pres
636	Kemnal College - Bromley South	Stagecoach	TB	Tri/ALX400
637	Kemnal College - Bromley South	Stagecoach	TB	Tri/ALX400
638	Coney Hall - Kemnal College	Stagecoach	TB	Tri/ALX400
639	Clapham Junction - Putney Heath John Paul II School	Go-Ahead	SW	B7TL/Gem B7TL/Pres
640	South Harrow - Clamp Hill	Arriva Shires	GR	DB300/Gem2
641	West Molesey - Teddington School	Quality Line	EB	Versa Dar/ALX200